D1087402

Jesús Fernández Santos

Twayne's World Authors Series

Janet Pérez, Editor of Spanish Literature

Texas Tech University

TWAS 687

JESÚS FERNÁNDEZ SANTOS
(1926–   )
Photograph courtesy of Miguel Fernández Castaldi

Jesús Fernández Santos

By David K. Herzberger

University of Connecticut, Storrs

Twayne Publishers • *Boston*

Jesús Fernández Santos

David K. Herzberger

Copyright © 1983 by G. K. Hall & Company
All Rights Reserved
Published by Twayne Publishers
A Division of G. K. Hall & Company
70 Lincoln Street
Boston, Massachusetts 02111

Book Production by Marne B. Sultz
Book Design by Barbara Anderson

Printed on permanent/durable acid-free
paper and bound in the United States of
America.

Library of Congress Cataloging in Publication Data

Herzberger, David K.
Jesús Fernández Santos.

(Twayne's world authors series; TWAS 687)
Bibliography: p. 126
Includes index.
1. Fernández Santos, Jesús—Criticism and
interpretation. I. Title. II. Series.
PQ6611.E657Z69   1983   863'.64   82-21228
ISBN 0-8057-6534-4

for Sharon

Contents

About the Author
Preface
Chronology

Chapter One
The Life and Times of Jesús Fernández Santos   1

Chapter Two
The Novels of Social Realism   11

Chapter Three
Existential Despair and the Individual   40

Chapter Four
Toward a Literature of Imagination   65

Chapter Five
Short Fiction   94

Chapter Six
Conclusion   117

Notes and References   121
Selected Bibliography   126
Index   129

About the Author

David K. Herzberger received the B.A. from the Pennsylvania State University and the M.A. and Ph.D. from the University of Illinois. He is currently associate professor of Spanish at the University of Connecticut, where he teaches undergraduate and graduate courses in nineteenth- and twentieth-century Spanish literature.

Professor Herzberger's major areas of research are the post–Civil War novel and modern narrative theory. In 1977 he was awarded a research fellowship from the American Council of Learned Societies to pursue research on the concept of the contemporary Spanish novel. He has published articles on the novel in journals such as *Hispanic Review, MLN, Symposium, Revista de Estudios Hispánicos, Hispania, Journal of Spanish Studies: Twentieth Century, Journal of Aesthetics and Art Criticism,* and *Studies in Twentieth Century Literature,* among others. He is also the author of *The Novelistic World of Juan Benet* and coeditor of *An Annual Bibliography of Post–Civil War Spanish Fiction.*

Preface

Jesús Fernández Santos falls chronologically into the group of Spanish novelists commonly known as the Generation of 1950. The realistic orientation and *engagé* approach to literature espoused by these writers (e.g., Juan Goytisolo, Juan García Hortelano, Luis Goytisolo, Rafael Sánchez Ferlosio) became the predominant literary force in Spain for nearly thirty years following the Spanish Civil War. Fernández Santos, however, has gained literary prestige not only because he published his first works during this period, but also because he initiated—as several critics and the author himself have pointed out—one of the principal tendencies associated with his generation: the novel of Social Realism (or Neo-realism), in which the major aim of the writer is to present with a critical vision the realities of contemporary society. With the publication of *Los bravos* [The Untamed] in 1954 Fernández Santos became a central figure in developing the Neo-realistic novel of the postwar period.

Fernández Santos has not remained stagnant within the literary tradition that he helped to create. He continued to embrace the precepts of Social Realism for more than a decade following the publication of *The Untamed*, but by the end of the 1960s his narrative development paralleled the general movement in Spain toward a more diversified mode of writing. His novels and short stories reflected a growing concern for the existential dilemma of individuals and, at the same time, embodied many of the innovative stylistic and technical devices aimed at enhancing the complexity of structure and language.

His most recent fiction further reveals his continued evolution as a writer. In direct contrast to his early works, which probe various aspects of contemporary Spanish society, his three most recent novels (*La que no tiene nombre* [The One Who Has No Name], *Extramuros* [Outside the Walls], and *Cabrera*) focus on life in Spain in the distant past and represent what the author himself terms a "literature of imagination." In short, the narrative trajectory of Fernández Santos reveals the growth and change of a writer who continually seeks to explore the multiple possibilities of his art form. As a result, Fernández Santos is one of the most versatile novelists of the postwar period, and also one of the best.

The present study represents an attempt to analyze the evolution of Fernández Santos's fiction from the early works of Social Realism to the present. I have employed an essentially eclectic critical methodology during the course of my analysis, although my point of departure is consistently the text itself rather than extra-aesthetic (e.g., biographical, political, historical, etc.) documents and ideas. I have identified in each of Fernández Santos's works of fiction the principal intrinsic norms that determine its literary mode of being. The evolution of his narrative is therefore viewed as an evolution of literary norms, and not as an integral part of the changing social and historical circumstances of postwar Spain.

During the course of my study I have divided Fernández Santos's fiction into different periods and genres. These divisions, however, should not be viewed as rigidly defined and mutually exclusive stages of development in the author's writing. On the contrary, many of the themes, techniques, and modes of characterization extend across different time periods. As occurs with nearly all writers, Fernández Santos does not move abruptly and completely from one literary phase to another, but remains linked to the past and its traditions.

I have excluded from my study Fernández Santos's film criticism, newspaper and magazine articles (some of which are collected in the book *Europa y algo más* [Europe and a Bit More], 1977), and film documentaries. Although his entire corpus of writings offers insight into his view of life and literature, his importance as a literary figure is due primarily to his prose fiction.

I would like to thank Jesús Fernández Santos for providing me with information about his life and works, and for consenting to a lengthy interview in Madrid in April of 1978. To Professor Janet Pérez I am indebted for offering me the opportunity to undertake this study for Twayne.

David K. Herzberger

University of Connecticut, Storrs

Chronology

1926   Jesús Fernández Santos born in Madrid.

1936   Civil War breaks out. Fernández Santos, vacationing with his family in San Rafael, is evacuated to Segovia.

1939   Returns to Madrid after Civil War.

1943–1948   Studies Liberal Arts at the University of Madrid. Acts in university theater groups. Participates in literary *tertulias* at the university and Café Gijón.

1949–1952   Studies at the Escuela Oficial de Cinematografía in Madrid. Embarks on film career.

1953   Collaborates in *Revista Española*.

1954   *Los bravos*.

1957   *En la hoguera* (awarded Gabriel Miró Prize).

1958   *Cabeza rapada* (awarded Critics' Prize).

1958–1969   Devotes most of his time to film and documentaries. Adapts novels and plays for Spanish National Television.

1959   Wins prizes of the Círculo de Escritores Cinematográficos and Sindicato Español del Espectáculo for documentary on Goya, *España, 1800*. Wins Premio de la Bienal de Venecia for documentary, *El Greco*.

1964   *Laberintos*.

1969   *El hombre de los santos* (awarded Critics' Prize). Returns to writing nearly full time. Severs relationship with the publisher Seix Barral.

1970   *Las catedrales*.

1971   *Libro de las memorias de las cosas* (awarded Nadal Prize and City of Barcelona Prize). Lectures at the University of Salamanca.

1973   *Paraíso encerrado*.

1975   Francisco Franco dies.

1976   Joins Madrid daily, *El País*, as film critic.

1977   *Europa y algo más* and *La que no tiene nombre*.

1978   *Extramuros* (awarded National Literature Prize).

1979   *A orillas de una vieja dama*.

1981   *Cabrera*.

Chapter One
The Life and Times of Jesús Fernández Santos
Childhood and War

When civil war erupted in Spain in 1936, Jesús Fernández Santos was ten years old. He recalls very little of significance about his childhood before this time, except that he made frequent trips with his father to the mountains of León and Asturias in northern Spain. His father emigrated to Madrid from the small Leonese mountain town of Cerulleda early in the 1900s, and in later years returned there with his family to visit relatives and friends. As did many other young persons of his generation, Fernández Santos's father had sought to escape the isolation and economic hardship of rural Spain and had moved to Madrid in search of work and financial gain. After living with relatives for several years and working at a variety of jobs, he managed to save enough money to open a small furniture store in Madrid and was able to enjoy many of the comforts of Spain's small, but growing, middle class.

The start of the Civil War in July of 1936 marked a decisive juncture in Fernández Santos's life, as it did for nearly all Spaniards. While vacationing in the town of San Rafael some thirty-five miles northwest of Madrid, the family learned that war had broken out and that the entire area was under control of the Nationalist (Franco) troops. Since the front was only a few miles to the east of San Rafael, everyone was to be evacuated to Segovia until it was safe to return to Madrid. Although Jesús and his family had only their summer clothes with them and enough money to last for a week, they were hardly concerned about their plight. Most of the people in Segovia assured them that the war would end quickly and that the Nationalist army would soon defeat the much weaker Republican forces. The writer recalls that, upon his arrival in Segovia, he saw Spanish youths going off to battle, singing and cheering for a Nationalist victory. Many of them were only fifteen or sixteen years old, and they marched through the streets wearing medals and hearts of Jesus. Fernández Santos vividly remembers that the young soldiers were captivated by the gaiety of the events and confident they would win the war in a few days. After a few weeks, however, the magnitude of the conflict began to emerge. The Republican forces did not surrender and the fighting was to last until March of 1939. The future novelist and his family were forced to remain in Segovia for nearly three years. Although the family did not experience severe hardship during this period, they lived with constant shortages of food and clothing and were obliged to sacrifice their personal needs for the war effort. The boy's father espoused generally conservative political views, but did not feel compelled to enlist in the Nationalist army. He was fifty-two years old at the time (too old to be drafted), but was called upon to perform civilian duties in Segovia for the Nationalist forces, and often served as a guard at the city prison. Since his three sisters worked as volunteers in hospitals and on food lines, Jesús was left alone much of the time to fend for himself. It was during this period of solitude that he began to read extensively. Although his parents had few books at home, he read magazines and newspapers and sought reading materials from neighbors and family friends.

The war years represented for Fernández Santos more of an inconvenience than a direct threat to his well-being. He does not recall witnessing violent or bloody deaths in Segovia, but remembers the frequent air raids, his family hurrying to reach the nearest bomb shelter, and the siren in the bell tower of the cathedral warning of approaching enemy planes. The constant interruption of his schooling and the ever-present possibility of danger, however, make the three years in Segovia critical to the writer's development. His recollections of the fighting, of stories that he was told about the events at the front, and his own vague sensations of fear appear in several of his short stories written in later years.

Shortly after the end of the war in 1939 Jesús and his family returned to Madrid, where the boy was immediately enrolled in a private Catholic school. Although very conservative and strict, the private schools offered by far the best education available during the postwar years, and students were drilled in Catholic dogma and traditional studies of the humanities. [1] Jesús continued to read as much as possible, but had access to relatively few books. At school his reading was limited to Spanish classics and religious works, and he was forced to borrow books secretly from his friends and a few close relatives. His father died in 1941 shortly after reestablishing his business affairs, and the adolescent Jesús was cared for by his older sisters. Although the family did not suffer from extreme poverty during the early years of the 1940s, like most residents of Madrid they constantly lacked food and other necessities. Nearly everything was rationed, and the writer recalls standing in long lines for bread, oil, and rice.

Early Literary Development

Fernández Santos's interest in literature was enhanced dramatically in 1943 when he enrolled in the College of Philosophy and Letters at the University of Madrid. The literary arts were again beginning to flourish at the university following the sterility of the war years, and students sought to fashion an atmosphere of creativity and intellectual discussion. Although political debate scarcely existed,[2] several theater and poetry groups were formed. In addition, despite strict government regulation of foreign literature, novels from Europe and the United States circulated freely among the students. Fernández Santos soon became active in literary *tertulias* and made his first important contact with several young writers (e.g., Ignacio Aldecoa, Alfonso Sastre, Rafael Sánchez Ferlosio, Alfonso Paso, Medardo Fraile) who were to become his longtime friends as well as important influences in his subsequent literary development. The group met frequently to discuss literature and film, and also shared translations of Hemingway, Steinbeck, Faulkner, and Dos Passos. Fernández Santos's later interest in writing about life outside large cities can be traced to his reading of many of these American writers, in particular Faulkner and Steinbeck.

During his five years at the University of Madrid (1943–1948) Fernández Santos organized and directed a theater group called *Arte Nuevo* that performed the works of Spanish and foreign dramatists such as Benavente, Strindberg, Goldoni, and Williams. Fernández Santos also wrote his first literary work during this period, a play entitled *Mientras cae la lluvia* [While the Rain Falls].[3] He both directed and acted in the play, which was produced at the university theater without much success. The theater group was later forced to disband, however, when they attempted to perform Federico García Lorca's *The House of Bernarda Alba* in defiance of university and government suppression of the work. Also during this period Fernández Santos pursued his literary interests outside the university. He spent much of his time at the Ateneo (temporarily renamed Aula de Cultura following the war), reading mostly nineteenth-century Spanish literature that had been excluded from his Catholic education.

Fernández Santos abandoned the university in 1948 without receiving his degree. Beset by financial problems, and concluding that his study of literature and philosophy would not provide future economic stability,

he enrolled in the newly opened Escuela Oficial de Cinematografía
(Official School of Cinema Arts) in 1949. In order to earn a living during
these years he worked for Radio Madrid in the theater department and
directed and acted in works by both Spanish and foreign playwrights.
For the most part, Fernández Santos felt frustrated with his classes at the
film school and found them to be boring and uninstructive. He continued with his studies, however, because he was seriously interested in
filmmaking and the school offered the only access in all of Spain to
cameras and other cinematographic equipment. It was also during this
period that Fernández Santos became acquainted with aspiring directors
Carlos Saura and Luis Berlanga, with whom he has remained in close
contact over the years. In 1952, after three years at the school, Fernández
Santos graduated with the title of director, and began to make documentaries about Spanish art.

During the early 1950s Fernández Santos maintained close ties with
his friends from the university. Their daily discussions, however, had
moved from the school cafeteria to the Café Gijón, a popular meeting
place in Madrid for writers, actors, and artists. Fernández Santos recalls
the years at the Café Gijón with nostalgia, for during this period he and
many of his friends published their first stories and novels or saw their
first plays performed. Credit for discovering Fernández Santos and his
group of friends and aiding their literary careers must be given to
Antonio Rodríguez Moñino, a well-known scholar and publisher who
was interested in promoting the works of young Spanish writers. With
Moñino providing intellectual guidance and financial support, Ignacio
Aldecoa, Alfonso Sastre, and Rafael Sánchez Ferlosio founded in May
1953 the *Revista Española*, a literary magazine aimed at providing a
creative outlet for fledgling authors. Although the magazine published
only six issues before going out of business,[4] it provided several young
writers with their first opportunity to publish short narratives and plays.
In addition to the three editors mentioned above, and Fernández Santos,
who was a frequent contributor, the magazine published early works by
Carmen Martín Gaite, Medardo Fraile, José Luis Castillo Puche, and
Juan Benet, all of whom later became well-known literary figures.

The Literary Possibilities of Postwar Spain

The publication of *Revista Española* and several other innovative
literary magazines founded in the late 1940s and early 1950s clearly
enhanced the revitalization of Spanish literature. Editors discovered
talented young authors and supported their diversified approaches to

writing. Away from the literary periodicals, however, the Spanish writer faced several difficult problems. In the first place, few Spanish publishing houses were interested in editing the works of young writers. Older, more established Spanish authors were being published, but the majority of publishing firms were occupied with translations of foreign works. Fernández Santos recalls that during this time any small success in having a work seriously considered for publication was like "passing into Utopia."[5] In many instances, however, the phase following editorial acceptance proved to be even more difficult, for the work had to be approved by government censors. From 1938 until passage of the Law of the Press of 1966, the Franco regime could legally censor the arts and all forms of mass communication. Under the wartime Censorship Law of 1938, the government was granted complete control over the publishing industry during a state of siege, a condition that officially existed in Spain for twenty-eight years following the Civil War. Although a writer might not have his work suppressed completely, certain words or even entire segments might be eliminated. Thus writers had to weigh the potential acceptability of what they were preparing and formulate their work accordingly. Even then, the arbitrary nature of what was suppressed offered few guidelines, except the obvious prohibition of material that criticized Franco, Spain, or the Catholic Church.[6]

Once a work was approved for publication, the Spanish novelist of this period was confronted by an even more frustrating problem: the lack of a reading public. Although the advent of literary prizes during the 1940s and 1950s increased circulation, an influx of translations of popular foreign writers overwhelmed most contemporary Spanish works. Novels by authors such as Cecil Roberts, Vicky Baum, Pearl Buck, Stefan Zweig, and several others inundated the market and nearly obscured their Spanish counterparts.[7] This is not to say, of course, that Spanish novelists did not publish their works during this time. In general, however, their books did not sell well and few copies were printed, often only two or three hundred.

Within this atmosphere of censorship, limited publishing outlets, and a generally disinterested reading public, Fernández Santos and his contemporaries wrote their early works of fiction. After several short stories appeared in *Revista Española* and other literary periodicals, Fernández Santos published his first novel, *Los bravos* [The Untamed], in 1954. Although the work was ranked a finalist in the important Nadal competition in 1951, Fernández Santos was unable to find a publisher for it until 1954, when Editorial Castalia began a ten-volume series of Spanish novels under the direction of Antonio Rodríguez Moñino. As literary historians have subsequently pointed out, *The Untamed* stands as a significant contribution to postwar Spanish literature, primarily because it begins a cycle of writing in Spain commonly termed Neo-realism or Social Realism. Nearly all the major novels of the 1950s follow the pattern of Social Realism, and an entire generation of writers emerged while adhering to the basic precepts associated with it. The brand of fiction developed by these writers was fundamentally a literature of denunciation: it examined the social and economic conditions of contemporary Spain and implicitly criticized poverty, oppression, and social injustice. The development of style and technique was subordinated to thematic concerns, while the accurate representation of reality superseded artistry as the principal task of the writer.

Several factors contributed to the development of Social Realism in Spain during the 1950s. Some literary historians suggest that it represented a return to the tradition of realism that characterizes a large portion of Spanish literature. Other critics point to the influence of the American "Lost Generation" and to the Neo-realistic orientation of postwar Italian film. Still others contend that the novel during this period became a means for portraying many of the social and economic ills that were precluded from discussion in newspapers and magazines.[8] While all of these factors no doubt contributed to the cultivation of Social Realism during the 1950s, Fernández Santos offers a more personal explanation for his manner of writing in *The Untamed*. During the Civil War, and extending throughout the decade of the 1940s, Fernández Santos felt excluded from the mainstream of Spanish life and from decisions regarding the present and future welfare of Spain. This exclusion eventually helped shape his early approach to writing: "[It was] a war in which we didn't matter. . . . That concrete sensation of not counting, of not formulating one's own destiny . . . began then and still continues. Perhaps because of that, because of the lack of any real participation, there grew in us a desire to transform a world, which was alien and inaccessible, into something closer to our own measure of it. . . . Because to write is both to create and to dominate; to assimilate experience and express it through one's own personality, at once transforming and expounding upon it; that is, re-creating it."[9]

Although *The Untamed* received a favorable critical response, it sold only a few hundred copies and fell far short of affording its author immediate literary fame. Two years later, in 1956, Fernández Santos published his second novel, *En la hoguera* [In the Fire]. Again, despite the critical success of the work, Fernández Santos was unable to support himself with his writing. Even his frequent contributions to newspapers and magazines did not diminish his economic hardship. In an interview in 1959, he lamented that "being a novelist in Spain is painful because of the limited economic possibilities of the novel. . . . Writing for newspapers pays very little. It's incomprehensible that newspapers are still paying two hundred pesetas for an article."[10]

Fernández Santos has voiced displeasure throughout his career with the small reading public for Spanish novelists, the limited printings of books (normally 4,000 copies in the first edition), and the ineffective advertising campaigns aimed at publicizing new works. Although it would be unfair to conclude that Fernández Santos is singularly preoccupied with economic success, he has continued to express his disappointment that few Spanish novelists can earn a living solely by writing. His concern with the public's lack of interest in Spanish writers has led him at times to appear callous, or to possess what some have termed an obsession with middle-class materialism. In 1969, for example, shortly after the publication of his novel *El hombre de los santos* [The Man of the Saints], Fernández Santos was questioned about his outlook on life. He responded, "My present posture can be summed up in four lines from a poem by Antonio Machado: 'And in the end, I owe you nothing, you owe me for what I have written / I attend to my work; I pay with my money for / the jacket that covers me and the house that I inhabit / the bread that nourishes me and the bed in which I lie.' "[11] In the same interview, when asked, "What is literature for you?" he cynically remarked, "As I said before, certainly not a way of making money. . . . A cause for vanity? What vanity can there be when four thousand persons in a country of thirty-five million read your work over a period of ten years? I would say that whoever writes seriously in Spain, out of vanity or to earn a living, will suffer physically and spiritually."

Fernández Santos clearly desires to be read and known by the Spanish public. In 1969 he severed his relationship with the important Barcelona publisher Seix Barral, primarily because the company was making extensive promotional efforts for its Latin American writers and devoting comparably scant attention to Spanish novelists.[12] When asked about the popularity of Latin American novelists in Spain, Fernández Santos responded that "I am not certain what is the magical formula that will enable us to confront the Latin American challenge. What I am sure of is that any formula will have to take into account the public. If we move away from the public, we novelists will end up like the poets: reading one another, or like the writers of the *nouveau roman*, who, according to their editor, are the most critically praised and least read writers in France."[13] But Fernández Santos by no means wishes to be viewed as a purely commercial author who writes mass-consumption novels in order to maintain a high standard of living. Instead, he hopes that the Spanish reading public will develop a greater literary sophistication and acquire an interest in contemporary Spanish literature as it is conceived by its most talented creators. Fernández Santos is aware that such a transformation can only occur over an extended period of time, but he believes that it has already begun and will continue to aid Spanish writers in the future.

Literature and Film

Soon after the financial failure of his second novel in 1956, Fernández Santos began to devote nearly all of his time to film. His work as a director spans the period from 1952 to the early years of the 1970s and includes nearly two hundred documentaries, one full-length film, and several television programs. His first major documentary, *España, 1800*, examines the life and times of Goya and was awarded two major prizes: the Premio del Círculo de Escritores Cinematográficos and the Premio del Sindicato Español del Espectáculo in 1959. His other documentaries include studies of Spanish painters, architecture, and museums, as well as films on Spanish life in different regions of the Iberian Peninsula. His only full-length film, *Llegar a más* [Getting Ahead], took five years to complete but resulted in critical indifference and financial loss. Fernández Santos recalls that the film was a difficult undertaking, one that he regrets having ever attempted. He wrote the script as well as directed the film and regards the project as "five years that were lost out of my life."[14]

During the late 1950s and the 1960s Fernández Santos expanded his work into Spanish National Television, where he directed several novel and play adaptations and wrote and directed documentaries on Spanish museums, contemporary writers, and historical events. His work earned him several awards as well as the respect of his colleagues in the film profession. More importantly, however, it provided him with the necessary financial stability to be able to return nearly full time to writing. Of course, Fernández Santos continued to write while he worked in film and television, but his literary output was limited to a collection of short stories, *Cabeza rapada* [Shaved Head, 1958], and a novel entitled *Laberintos* [Labyrinths], published in 1965. Since 1969, however, Fernández Santos has become one of the most prolific writers in Spain, and his fiction has won broad critical and public recognition. He currently resides in a fashionable section of Madrid, and has again begun to participate in *tertulias* at the Café Gijón. Cinema continues to interest him, and he writes film criticism for the Madrid daily *El País*.

Although financial success was an important by-product of Fernández Santos's work in film and television, his travels during the 1950s and 1960s provide a backdrop for much of his later narrative. While making documentaries Fernández Santos journeyed throughout Spain. He grew more familiar with his country's cultural traditions and became acquainted with persons and local tales that were to provide the impetus for many of his short stories and novels. Fernández Santos adheres to the general writing philosophy that the novelist should understand fully his native surroundings and reflect this knowledge in his writing. He asserted in an interview in 1959, for example, that "the novel should be . . . an interpretation of the country in which we live, a personal interpretation that stems from an intimate knowledge of [what is Spanish]."[15]

Fernández Santos demonstrates a profound knowledge of Spain in many of his works, especially in those that re-create incidents from his travels. *Libro de las memorias de las cosas* [The Book of Memorable Events, 1971], for example, a novel about a small Spanish Protestant sect, stems directly from the author's visit to the mountains of northern Spain, where by chance he passed by two Protestant gravesites outside a tiny village. Characters and scenes from *Las catedrales* [The Cathedrals, 1970] also reflect the author's travels, as does the general ambience of *The Untamed* and *La que no tiene nombre* [The One Who Has No Name, 1977]. More concretely, the principal character of *The Man of the Saints* originates with a person whom Fernández Santos met when filming a documentary on the transfer of paintings from an ancient convent in Zamora to a museum in Toledo. Fernández Santos relates that, while at work on the project, "I met an elderly man, a historical leftover from a profession, half technician and half artisan. Like me, that man traveled the roads of the Peninsula. . . . Also like me, he worked in a nomadic sort of profession that offered a certain independence. I took him as the subject for a novel, as the principal character, and made him in body and soul move about Spain; in body, throughout the Peninsula, in soul, throughout my entire lifetime."[16] In this instance, Fernández Santos not only molds his character around a real-life figure but identifies with the character as a reflection of his own psychological makeup.

The geographic area of Spain that provides the background for several of Fernández Santos's short stories and two of his novels (*The Untamed* and *The One Who Has No Name*) lies approximately two hundred miles to the northwest of Madrid in the mountains of León and Asturias. As a child Fernández Santos made frequent visits to these mountains with his father, and since then he has filmed documentaries about the people of the area. He owns a house in the town where his father once lived and spends a few months there each year, writing and walking among the hills. Fernández Santos is drawn to the mountains and the people of northern León partly because of emotional ties ("Part of my life is there," he maintains)[17] and partly out of curiosity to discover more about the region. Most of the small mountain villages now consist of only a few stone houses and farms, since many of the young adults have emigrated to larger cities. During the winter the communities are totally isolated from one another and only recently, with the installation of electricity and television antennas, have they had any connection with the rest of the country during the snowy months of fall and winter. Fernández Santos's familiarity with this isolated area, as well as with several other remote regions of the Peninsula, has led him to view the Spanish character as shaped by a kind of geographic determinism. Thus, for example, he characterizes the Asturians as extroverted and carefree (they lead a hard life as miners), while the Leonese are portrayed as introverted and cautious (they are farmers in a hostile climate). In nearly all of his fiction the intensity and depth of the narrative result from the commingling of character and environment. His novels explore both universal and uniquely Spanish themes, but these are always submerged in a profoundly Spanish ambience with which Fernández Santos is intimately acquainted.

Chapter Two
The Novels of Social Realism

Los bravos

During the 1950s in Spain social consciousness emerged as the most compelling motive for the creation of narrative fiction. The novel became the most important literary vehicle for social and political protest, although direct criticism of Spanish society was precluded to a large degree by government censorship. Fernández Santos's contributions to the novel during this period are identified both with the origins of Social Realism and its subsequent evolution during the 1950s into the dominant literary mode of the decade. Although his first work, *Los bravos* [The Untamed, 1954], did not stimulate widespread public or critical interest (it sold only a few hundred copies), Alberto Gil Novales of *Insula* termed it "a splendid novel" and linked it to the generation of young writers striving to interpret in their fiction diverse elements of contemporary Spanish life.[1] During the late 1950s and early 1960s, however, *The Untamed* began to receive wider critical attention as other writers published novels with similar thematic and technical constructs, and Social Realism emerged as a well-defined literary movement with specific norms and intentions. Fernández Santos in fact has suggested that with *The Untamed* he invented Social Realism in Spain, and many literary historians now recognize the work as the first major example of this particular brand of fiction in postwar Spanish literature.

Fernández Santos sets the action of *The Untamed* in an unnamed village located in northern León, a short distance from the mountains that divide the provinces of León and Asturias. Fernández Santos's father grew up in the mountains of that area, and the author himself often visited there during his youth. Since Fernández Santos opted for a realistic brand of fiction for his first novel, it was logical for him to examine a way of life that he knew intimately: "For the writing of my first novel I chose a region, a town that I knew well and for which I felt something . . . I knew the area and its people well, their past, their present and also—I believe now—their future. They moved me, and that is how I tried to deal with them [in my novel]."[2]

The detailed representation of daily life and the monotonous existence of the people who inhabit the small town are the clear focal points of *The Untamed*. Hence, rather than concentrate on a few principal characters, Fernández Santos offers a collective protagonist by moving a wide variety of persons in and out of the narrative. Little attempt is made at traditional plot development, since the novel relates a series of random activities in the town during the summer months of the late 1940s. The events of the novel are linked structurally both by the physical presence of the town and by the movements of a young doctor who has recently arrived in the area and visits many of the townspeople. Several characters are introduced during the course of the narrative, but very little happens to change their lives or to suggest that they will ever escape their dreary existence. Fernández Santos does create, however, a limited amount of intrigue in the novel: the doctor steals the mistress of Don Prudencio, the town's wealthiest landowner; a stranger passes through the village and convinces the people that he is a bank representative who can provide them with a secure future. The stranger subsequently absconds with their money but is later captured and returned to the town for punishment. For the most part, however, the narrator offers an objective view of life in this particular region of rural Spain, underscoring the physical and spiritual poverty of the persons who live there.

Milieu

Fernández Santos is well aware that realistic fiction must stem in large part from milieu. Thus character portrayal in *The Untamed* is subordinated to the regionalist flavor of small-town life. Even more importantly, however, the author affirms in his novel the influence of geographic determinism and submerges his characters in an atmosphere of tedium and abulia from which they cannot hope to escape.[3] Fernández Santos underscores the function of milieu from the outset of the novel. The reader's first view of the town is focused on the desolate landscape and a small mass of decrepit buildings nearly devoid of life: "The town was empty. The houses, the river, the bridges and the road seemed deserted like always, as if their only purpose was to exist for themselves, without serving as places to live or means of transportation."[4] Everything about the town contributes to the pervasive feeling of emptiness and abandonment. The church stands in ruins, the houses are poorly constructed, and the town no longer has a priest. Thus it is suggested that even God has abandoned the village to its misery.

The impact of nature also intensifies the sense of hostility and isolation of the area. The narrator repeatedly calls attention to the burning sun that makes work intolerable during the midday hours, and the characters frequently discuss the "unbearable heat," or the "heat, sun, and sweat" of their everyday existence. The winter months are equally destructive, however, for heavy snows compel the people to remain in their houses for several weeks at a time. This sense of isolation is intensified by the mountain ranges surrounding the village and by the few visitors that pass through the town. Furthermore, the infertile land fails to provide the residents of the village with any hope of earning enough money to escape the area, and each year the meager harvest continues to diminish. Through the accumulation of descriptive fragments and recurring allusions to the geographic and natural elements of the milieu, Fernández Santos provides a deterministic backdrop for the portrayal of his villagers. Of course, other factors help to shape the characters and their perceptions of life, but Fernández Santos underscores throughout his narrative the impingement of the physical milieu upon the spiritual and psychological makeup of the townspeople.

The isolation or insulation of the village from the outer world is also suggested in the novel through the portrayal of time. The characters and the town itself are suspended in an atmosphere where change has ceased. Outer time (i.e., time outside the hamlet) moves on, but the sense of duration within the town disperses into emptiness and no longer exists. The notion of temporal paralysis is affirmed at the outset of the novel by the description of the clock on the church tower. The hands of the clock were broken during the Civil War, and since then the pueblo has stood in a rarefied atmosphere of stagnation. Nothing has altered the daily routine of village life, and the townspeople endure a vacuous existence without hope of progress. This isolation from external time, however, does not function as a form of preservation or protection from the destructive consequences of temporal duration. The town sinks further into decay as the years pass: the church continues to deteriorate, the soil grows less fertile, and the young adults of the area emigrate to large cities in search of work. In one sense, therefore, the town is cut off from the constructive potential of progress and the forward movement of time. Yet it also suffers from the destruction that accompanies temporal flow.

That time indeed moves in a positive fashion outside the village is confirmed by the brief scenes that portray Prudencio's visit to the provincial capital: "[Prudencio] left the station behind. He was already in the capital. This was the place to live: smooth streets, bars, theaters, well-dressed people, automobiles, and flowerpots shining atop the streetlights all along the avenues. . . . He didn't understand business, but he understood why the young people struggled to come to the capital, why they abandoned the land and their families in order to come here to live" (129–130). Life in the city thus symbolizes progress, development, and activity and stands in direct contrast to small-town decadence and isolation.

The milieu of *The Untamed* takes on deeper meaning, of course, as a series of specifically dimensioned characters gradually appear within it. None of the characters, however, is developed with any importance attached to psychological profundity. Individuals emerge only to the extent that they are identified with certain social positions or with common dilemmas. Since the prevailing technique of the novel is one of observation and reportage, along with occasional impressionistic or pseudopoetic descriptions of nature, the characters come alive by their actions and words, and only occasionally is the reader permitted to view internal motivations and thought processes. What results from this kind of broad representation, then, is the development of a collective protagonist that reifies the essence of rural life.

Characters

Several characters of *The Untamed* are linked to social problems (e.g., poverty, injustice), while others are portrayed in relation to a specific personal dilemma, such as love or family tragedy. In each instance, the character's conflict either originates in or is intensified by the town, which determines to a large degree the character of the people confined both physically and psychologically within it. For example, Antón, the municipal secretary, feels trapped in his marriage to a chronically ill and overweight wife who constantly pursues him around town. While at times the marriage borders on caricature and farce, a more profound problem emerges when the reader is offered a brief glimpse of Antón's thoughts: "What would his life have been like if he hadn't married? At times he felt like protesting like a little child. Why had time changed everything? His wife laughed when she was young and she had a warm and elegant body when he courted her in another town, a long time ago. Everything passed in a flash, in a few years, in a day" (174). Temporal progression has ceased to function for Antón on a psychological plane. It is as if chronological measurement of time, such as days, weeks, and years, were diluted, and only a personal time remains, marked by the relentless quarreling with his wife.

The plight of Amador's son is equally tragic. The child has been bedridden for four years, and none of a series of doctors has been able to cure him. The boy's only respite from his tedious existence occurs during his hours of sleep, when he is freed from thought and is able to escape his agony. The young boy is clearly linked to the town in two important ways: he lives isolated from those around him (like the town as a whole), and at the same time his continuing illness can be attributed to the lack of special treatment that would be available in large cities. The sickness of the boy thus enhances the central theme of isolation on both a physical and psychological level.

The most pathetic figure of the novel, however, and the one most intensely conscious of her irresolvable dilemma, is Amparo. Amparo's life consists mainly of caring for her mother, who has not left her bed since her husband failed to return from the Civil War. Amparo's view of the world is clearly molded by her isolation from life outside the village, as well as by her conviction that she will never be happy. When the stranger arrives in town and boards with Amparo and her mother, the young woman has an affair with him. This ephemeral gratification, however, only serves ultimately to underscore Amparo's plight: "Year after year. At night she went to bed battered, tired, without knowing against what or against whom to rebel; then to move around hour after hour all day, like the mule at the well who didn't understand the purpose of what he was doing" (155). The symbol of the captive mule moving in circles and the reference to hours, days, and years reaffirms the inevitable failure of Amparo's existence. The continuum of time in her life is marked by intensity only, and is divorced from length and pace. Like the mule turning the waterwheel while walking in circles, her life has no movement apart from the daily pattern of tedium.

The existential dilemma of Amparo is not fully developed, for she is only one element of the collective mentality that eventually emerges in the novel. Yet Amparo represents more than any other character the fundamental problem of stagnation that Fernández Santos probes repeatedly in his work: "Seated by the window, she looked at the men laughing. She let the sun shine on her body, so that it burned to the point of overwhelming her in a sensation of annihilation and emptiness; only then did she move into the shade of the porch. It was like her life: a slow progression toward nothingness, amid faraway echoes of pain, boredom and desire" (227). This progression toward nothingness, and the accompanying paralysis of human activity, affirm the principal thematic concern of the narrative: the abulia and resignation of the town on a collective level. In the epigraph that prefaces the novel Fernández Santos suggests through a quotation from Jacob Wasserman the basic principle that he will examine in his work: "The destiny of a town is like the destiny of a man. Its character is its destiny." Viewed in its totality, the novel stands as a penetrating exploration of a people's character, and it relates how this character indeed becomes destiny.

The inactivity and tedium burdening the pueblo and its inhabitants take on broader social significance when other incidents and characters are examined. The poverty of the town, for example, is further underscored by the marriage of Antonio to a woman from a nearby village. While the wedding itself inspires festive celebration and offers a break from routine, spirits are gloomy among those who contemplate the couple's future. As one of the townspeople remarks to the doctor: "'You'll see when they begin to have children. It would be better if they weren't born. . . . ''Why?' Alfredo had turned around and was looking at him firmly, almost angrily. 'To suffer hunger and misery all their lives, that's why they got married'" (150).

The inevitable poverty experienced by nearly all of the townspeople leads directly to the theme of emigration in the novel. Small towns in rural Spain have been decreasing in population for much of the twentieth century because young adults move to large cities in search of work and financial gain. Those who abandon their towns rarely return, hence many villages simply cease to exist when their older inhabitants die. In *The Untamed*, although the problem of emigration is mentioned in several instances, it centers for the most part on Pepe, a young worker who drives the municipal van, transporting supplies from a larger town a few hours away. That Pepe is the character who chooses to emigrate is highly significant, for his brief daily encounters with life outside the town foster a desire for accomplishment. In contrast to most other characters in the novel, who perpetuate the status quo, Pepe escapes the deterministic elements of his milieu by asserting his will. Although his chances for success seem slim (he hopes to own a bar), the act of self-assertion is more meaningful in this case than the final outcome of his efforts.

The two characters linked most directly to the destiny of the town are Don Prudencio, who dominates life in the area because of his wealth, and a young doctor who has recently taken up residence there. Prudencio functions in the novel on two levels: first, he is the principal landowner of the village and thus exercises direct economic control over the inhabitants. He rents land to the local farmers and influences municipal government. He also owns the largest house and has as his mistress the most beautiful woman of the area. Prudencio is the target of scorn and resentment not simply for his wealth, but because he has never had to toil in the fields in order to earn his money. As Pepe notes: "'Sometimes you think it's because of his money, but other people are richer than he is, and you can tolerate them. It may be because we have never seen him work at anything.' 'At nothing?' 'At nothing'"(17–18). In contrast, the other inhabitants of the town "work an entire lifetime for nothing" (19).

More important than his economic and political influence, however, Prudencio stands as a symbol of psychological oppression that the townspeople are unwilling or afraid to challenge. The well-being of the town depends to a large degree on Prudencio, and his decisions are intimately related to the future of the inhabitants. He thus becomes a figure whose mere presence weighs upon the hopes of the people and oppresses their vitality. Prudencio scorns the town ("What a miserable town! A row of houses on either side of the river and nothing more. What a miserable town!" [95]), and the people are clearly aware of his view of them. Yet there is no spirit of rebellion among the villagers, or even a belief that the situation can be altered, that the power of Prudencio can be diluted. Prudencio thus serves in the novel not only to advance the tenuous plot, but also to intensify the principal thematic preoccupation: that is, that the destiny of a people (as Wasserman affirms) stems directly from their character. Because of their abulia the villagers are indeed doomed to remain under the economic and psychological domination of Prudencio or a figure like him.

It is in this light that the role of the young doctor must be examined. For the most part, the doctor (who remains nameless) functions in the work as a structural device: his presence links many of the scenes and enables the diverse actions of the novel to take place. As the work develops, however, the doctor emerges as a central figure in the thematic progression. The reader knows little about the doctor's life before his arrival, but the narrator hints at an unsettled past: "He had fled from the city to the town, and now he was fleeing from the town also" (185). During his first few months in the village the doctor remains aloof from the mainstream of events, visiting patients and becoming acquainted with the residents. But his participation in two important incidents that affect Prudencio and the town intensifies dramatically the thematic linking of destiny and collective character. The first of these incidents centers on Socorro, Prudencio's mistress. Prudencio views the young woman as a symbol of his wealth and position in the town, and regards her as one of his most valuable possessions. The doctor's first contact with Prudencio stems from the latter's preoccupation with Socorro's health. The doctor is called upon to examine her, and the brief encounter between the two eventually leads to Socorro's abandonment of Prudencio in order to live with the doctor.

There can be little doubt that the doctor is attracted emotionally to
Socorro, yet he desires to possess her as an affront to Prudencio as well, as
is clearly demonstrated by the portrayal of the doctor's thoughts both
before and after Socorro moves in with him. While examining her for the
first time, the doctor resents Prudencio's presence and his control over
the woman: "Don Prudencio entered without knocking. It was an
unpleasant way of showing his authority in the house, and the doctor was
about to tell him so, but instead he picked up his bag and got ready to
leave. He thought: 'I already knew she belonged to him, this wasn't
necessary'"(52). When he and Socorro move into their new house,
however, the doctor regards her as his: "Socorro sat down at the other
side of the table. There he had her, his now; she belonged to him, and
there was no reason to torment himself thinking about Don Prudencio"
(143). His possession of Socorro (and therefore of a part of Prudencio's
prestige) marks the first step in the doctor's increasingly active role in
the town, forming part of the process through which he will eventually
assume both the actual and symbolic position of Don Prudencio.

The doctor's chance encounter with the stranger who has defrauded the
townspeople of their savings motivates the final sequences of the novel
and solidifies the doctor's role in the town. While returning from a trip
into the mountains the doctor comes upon the stranger, who has been
captured and beaten in a nearby village and is being returned to the
defrauded town. The doctor is certain that the prisoner will be mis-
treated and offers to deliver the man directly to Amador, the municipal
president. When the doctor returns with the prisoner, the townspeople
demand that he be turned over to them. Despite the angry protests of the
crowd the doctor refuses, and delivers the prisoner to Amador the
following morning. What is most significant about this episode, of
course, is the doctor's defiance of the townspeople and his reasons for
acting as he does. He first thinks that perhaps he is a truly charitable
person, but concludes that it is easy to be charitable when one has not
lost his money to the swindler. Above all, however, the doctor realizes
that he cannot continue to live on the fringes of the town's society, that
he must take a position. He therefore becomes embroiled in a problem
that will certainly inspire animosity. Indeed, when he defies the wishes
of the townspeople, they respond by ostracizing him: he is forced to
move out of his rented house, no one in the town will speak to him, and
Socorro is unable to buy food. Faced with the dilemma of abandoning the
town (as he did the city before) or staying on despite the pressure, the
doctor chooses to remain. This act of defiance clearly confounds the

townspeople and intensifies their hostility. Later, when Prudencio dies of a heart attack and his estate is auctioned, the doctor buys his house. He thereby claims the final symbolic trappings of Prudencio's position and fulfills the latter's role in the town on both a psychological and physical level.

There is some dispute among critics concerning the final role of the doctor in the novel. Pablo Gil Casado, for example, argues that the doctor has become the new *patrón* of the town,[5] while Gonzalo Sobejano and Gregorio Martín contend that the doctor has been portrayed as a kind, charitable individual who is not of the temperament to assume the role of Prudencio.[6] Although not explicitly enunciated within the narrative, it seems clear that the novel is structured so as to delineate the doctor's usurpation of Prudencio's position. As previously discussed, the doctor first secures a portion of Prudencio's prestige when he gains possession of Socorro. Following this incident, the doctor opposes the town (as only Prudencio has done before) by aiding the swindler. When the doctor travels to a nearby town in order to buy food, one of the persons in the bar remarks, "'And they say that [the doctor] doesn't know what he's doing; in a few years that guy will own the town'" (217). Finally, the doctor assumes control of Prudencio's house (the largest in the municipality), and the narrator draws a direct parallel between the two characters. Earlier in the novel we learn that Prudencio enjoyed sitting on the balcony of his house, where he could view the town below: "From the semidarkness behind the venetian blind he could see the town at his feet, the double row of houses on both sides of the river, springing up from the brown dry land" (83). In precisely the same fashion at the end of the novel the doctor positions himself on the balcony: "The doctor went out on the balcony. He pulled up a chair and, sitting down, he contemplated the town at his feet" (236).

This is not to say, of course, that the doctor will accumulate the wealth of Prudencio, or that he will become a calculating, derisive landlord. The doctor is a "foreigner" in the town, however, and is obliged either to accommodate the townspeople completely or to oppose them and their abulic acceptance of life. Eventually, when compelled to make a series of decisions, the doctor opts to be banished from village society in order to assume the role of Don Prudencio. Thus the end of the novel returns the reader to the very beginning. The inhabitants of the town will continue to be dominated by the figure in the big house and will endure a life of resignation and hatred. Viewed in this light, then, the doctor serves to enhance structural unity and sustain thematic intensity.

Technique

The theoretical constructs of the social novel in Spain during the
1950s take root in the subordination of artistic performance to the social
or moral responsibility of the writer. Technique is determined by
thematic concerns, and the primary role of literary language is simply to
communicate as accurately as possible the particular reality at hand. In
The Untamed, Fernández Santos explores specific dimensions of life in a
rural Spanish town, and his principal technique reflects the intent to
represent this reality in a comprehensive and straightforward manner.
First of all, he constructs his narrative around the observations of a
third-person omniscient narrator, who witnesses the activities of the
town and offers an abundance of concrete details. As occurs in much of
his early fiction, the narrative often appears as if it were conveying life
through the eye of a camera, which is continually focused on the external
flow of social reality.[7] Fernández Santos is also aware, however, that
narrative description and exposition are less precise than immediate
presentation of action; thus much of the novel is comprised of dialogue
and direct interaction among the characters.

The Untamed has no chapter divisions, but rather consists of brief sequences in which various inhabitants of the town move about and carry on
their daily activities. Fernández Santos does not seek to create dramatic
pauses or emotional climaxes, but instead offers a continuous flow of
action as if his novel represented a true slice of life. As a result, the reader
is completely immersed in the town and is able to view nearly everything
that the inhabitants do: wake up in the morning, work in the fields, buy
food, celebrate a holy day, drink wine in the bar, etc. The novel thus
becomes a remarkably persuasive mimetic structure that conveys a real
sense of life and experience. At the same time, however, there is a
conscious shaping and structuring of the narrative in order to enhance
theme. The steady succession of short scenes demonstrates that there is
so little movement, so little change in the town, that the sense of tedium
and monotony intensifies without interruption. Inhabitants of the town
simply exist, and the eye of the narrator is present to record and organize.

Despite the overall objectivity of the narrative in *The Untamed*,
Fernández Santos occasionally offers a poetic view of the mountains and
surrounding countryside. For example, in one segment of the novel the
narrator records the movement of a dog as it walks through the town.
The point of view then shifts to the dog and the reader sees what the dog
is able to see at ground level. The narrator intervenes in the sequence,
however, in order to describe the nearby mountains that the dog has

overlooked: "Although he didn't see them, there were the blue mountains, bright with the sun close to setting, projecting long shadows from each spire, each crest, without a cloud covering their peaks. Brown in their foothills, blue at the summit, in eternal silence, broken only by a thousand small echoes, by the low of some solitary animal or the intermittent crackling of the shale. And on the other side, the moist vapor of the rivers, with the sea as a background, eternally enveloped in fog" (91—92). The narrator's sensitivity to nature is also revealed through the use of anthropomorphized images. A lake in the mountains is described as "That blue, watery, crystalline eye that commanded respect and inspired tales in everyone who came in contact with it" (191); the moon appears as "a large and white mother watching over her dark children asleep in the valley" (204); while the hot sun is able "to caress" (42) the face of one of the characters. That the narrator (rather than one of the characters) offers a poetic view of nature is significant here, because it suggests that the townspeople are incapable of enjoying the beauty that surrounds them. Although a large portion of the novel consists of dialogue, the characters never mention the landscape or the mountains except to curse the infertile soil or complain about the burning sun. The grandeur of their surroundings escapes the townspeople, burdened with the problem of survival and consumed by their hatred of Prudencio.

The intervention of the narrator is also evident through the creation of minor intrigue. The principal concern of the novel, as previously discussed, is to reveal the tedium and monotony of daily life in a rural village. Fernández Santos must be careful, though, to avoid one of the pitfalls of this kind of novel—that, while creating an atmosphere in which very little happens (i.e., he examines boredom), he does not write a boring novel. The novelist overcomes this problem through the use of intrigue. He does not set out, however, to fabricate a complex pattern of conflict among the characters or construct an entangled plot in the manner of a mystery novel, but rather creates intrigue through the simple technique of anticipation. For example, when a stranger arrives in town (44), there is no immediate explanation of his presence. Fernández Santos does not reveal the purpose of the stranger's visit, but rather allows curiosity to deepen for nearly sixty pages as the stranger talks with several of the townspeople and explains why he is there. In the meantime, several scenes and actions are interpolated into the developing subplots, and thus the suspense grows slowly and is sustained over a long period of narrative space. This same technique is used in several other instances as well: the portrayal of Prudencio's illness and eventual death; the relationship between the doctor and Socorro; Alfredo's passion for fishing illegally in the river. Thus while Fernández Santos effectively portrays the overwhelming sense of abulia that forms the nucleus of his novel, he maintains the interest of the reader by creating and sustaining intrigue through the gradual forward movement of minor drama. Although the author clearly intends to present a view of daily life in his novel, in the end he reaches an accommodation between the continuity of ongoing life and the literary requisites of structure and pace.

Fernández Santos introduces several minor themes in *The Untamed* that recur to some extent in his other fiction: the hazardous working conditions and poverty of miners in Asturias and León; the devastating physical and psychological effects of the Civil War, which accelerated the decadence of the town; the function of religion in small towns that have been abandoned by the Church. These themes appear at diverse points in the work and reinforce the more fundamental preoccupations of social injustice, poverty, and abulia. Viewed collectively, these concerns convey the central message of the novel that the tragedy of the town stems from the very fact that it exists.

En la hoguera

En la hoguera [In the Fire] was published in 1957, three years after *The Untamed*, and in many ways parallels the technique and thematic focus of the earlier novel. Life in rural Spain is again related with a concern for external detail, and several characters move in and out of the narrative in fragmented sequences that convey the collective mentality of village life. Also similar to his procedure in *The Untamed*, Fernández Santos creates a milieu that directly affects the psychological and physical existence of the characters, while economic hardship and social injustice are explored as a tragic corollary of the town's isolation and ruin. In contrast to *The Untamed*, however, *In the Fire* is constructed around the lives of two principal characters who incarnate the thematic concerns of the novel and whose thoughts and actions add structural unity to the narrative. Likewise in opposition to *The Untamed*, Fernández Santos probes psychological conflict more deeply in *In the Fire* and thereby achieves greater balance between the objective representation of external reality and the internal subjectivity of his characters.

The principal figure of *In the Fire* is Miguel, a young man in his mid-twenties suffering from tuberculosis. When Miguel realizes that his illness is growing worse, he decides to leave Madrid and travel through the small towns of Castille. As the reader follows the journey of Miguel through several provincial villages, the drama of Inés, the second major character, is developed in alternating chapters. After living with her aunt in Madrid for several months, Inés becomes pregnant by her cousin Agustín. When Agustín refuses to marry her, Inés attempts unsuccessfully to commit suicide. Following her recuperation she resolves to return to her home town (in rural Castille), even though she is aware that the stigma of her pregnancy will become more acute there. The stories of Inés and Miguel advance separately during the first eight chapters of the novel, but become intertwined in Chapter 9 when Miguel decides to spend the summer in Inés's town. During the remainder of the work the relationship between Miguel and Inés is developed more fully, and a variety of social and personal problems of the townspeople come into view. Following a pattern similar to that of his previous novel, therefore, Fernández Santos sketches a panoramic view of a provincial Spanish village, although he scrutinizes more closely in *In the Fire* the existential dilemma of the two principal characters.

The social and existential conflicts of *In the Fire* are developed in complementary fashion between individuals and the town as a whole. The social focus of the novel thus emerges in the same manner as in *The Untamed*: Fernández Santos underscores the role of geographic determinism by creating a milieu of isolation, poverty, and hostile physical surroundings; the disparity among social classes is clearly drawn in order to illustrate a specific injustice (in this case, the lack of medical treatment for the poor); unemployment undermines the economic structure of the town and generates massive emigration. Each of these problems, however, is subordinated to a more fundamental element that lies at the heart of the novel: the conflict between life and death embodied by Miguel and Inés. The atmosphere of the novel, both physical and psychological, serves to enhance the life/death antithesis, and the town itself functions as the principal locus for its development.

As in *The Untamed*, the town represented in *In the Fire* is located in a clearly defined geographic zone in North Central Spain. Miguel's journey in early spring through several small villages (Sepúlveda, Iscar, Sacramenia, Turégano, and Cantalejo) of the provinces of Soria and Segovia enables the narrator to provide an overview of the area within the limited framework of the plot. All of the towns that Miguel visits exist in "real life," and each is described to illustrate better the dominant features of isolation, poverty, and decadence. Consequently, the unnamed town in which Miguel finally settles takes on broad meaning as a well-defined representative of a provincial village, rather than as a unique or even abnormal example of rural Spanish life.

Each village portrayed in the novel is victimized by the destructive climatic conditions of the central Spanish plains. By the beginning of April, when Miguel decides to spend the summer in Inés's town, the heat of the day becomes so oppressive that the inhabitants fear their crops will be destroyed by July. As the summer progresses, the heat and drought cause the entire crop to be lost, and the residents of the area face the prospect of severe poverty and hunger. The narrator takes care to point out, however, that their hardship is not merely a result of the current drought, but rather constitutes the essence of life on the barren plain throughout its history. The principle of geographic determinism thus emerges in the novel as an important component of theme, and intensifies the feelings of despair that oppress the persons forced to live in the town. As the narrator observes concerning one of the women, "[Elena] realized that everything had always been the same: the pueblo and the empty plain, and the poor houses and the white sky."[8]

The village exemplifies the physical decadence characterizing much of rural Spain. The first view of the town, for example, describes a mass of crumbling houses seemingly devoid of life: "Beyond the bridge, at the top of the hill, a few houses sprang up, surrounded by the crumbling line of walls. Perhaps inside the walls there was something intact, but with the fading brilliance of twilight, the tenuous light from the windows illuminated only a pile of ruins" (93). Furthermore, the town no longer has a priest and the church stands abandoned. Yet the physical decay of the church merely symbolizes the more profound spiritual degeneration of the town as a whole. The bell on the church reminds a visiting priest that, for the townspeople, "God is going to die, that God has died" (147). The infinite extension of the plain intensifies the sense of isolation of the townspeople ("Beyond the walls the plain extended in all directions. On it, like a solitary peg in the brilliant atmosphere, floated the pueblo. The leaden walls seemed to embrace it blindly, and held it prisoner close to the plain" [142]), and the narrator suggests that the destiny of the people is determined not by God, but by the physical potency of the environment: "The reddish moon seemed to envelop the plain in a singular destiny, bloody, impossible to avoid, that affects all men equally" (170).

Nature Symbolism

The despair and abulia characterizing the general ambience of the novel are further enhanced by a series of images contrasting the forces of life and death. Apart from the portrayal of Miguel and Inés, the most decisive symbol of this conflict is linked directly to the meteorological conditions of the area. As the heat of the summer grows more intense and the drought continues, the river that flows by the town (i.e., the symbol of life) begins to dry up. By the end of the summer it no longer moves at all, and the water collects in stagnant pools. When the river ceases to flow, it is suggested, so will the pulse of the town. The water symbolism continues to appear throughout the narrative and contrasts with the heat and aridity of the plain. Eventually the town fountain runs dry, and nearly all of the men abandon their homes in order to work at the construction site of a dam several miles away. Fernández Santos thus suggests that the town itself will shortly cease to exist and the families will settle near the dam (i.e., water), where they will be able to sustain their existence on the "burning plain."

Another important symbol of the life/death contrast centers on the trees of the plain. Several decades before, the area was dotted with large groves of oak trees, but the need for more farm land eventually caused the trees' destruction. Now, however, neither the crops (i.e., annual rebirth) nor the trees (symbolic of sustained life) exist, and without the vegetation the plain appears as a sterile wasteland. Yet the narrator suggests that life will not completely vanish, but instead continue to endure. The notion of endurance or perseverance is crucial here, for it defines both the quality of life for the townspeople as well as the nature of existence on the plain as a whole. This dialectic between the dissolution of life and resistance to death is captured in the title of the novel. As Gonzalo Sobejano astutely observes, "To be 'in the fire' means being consumed, already dead yet still alive, part ash and part flame that still illuminates the ash, half in nothingness of extinction and half in the midst of burning."[9]

The significance of the trees is represented most clearly by the single cypress that stands outside the house of Elena and Baltasar: "On the burning plain, on the outskirts of the dying town gradually being buried by dust, the cypress is the only sign of life that endures" (122). The tree not only stands as an imposing symbol of the antithetical life/death forces of the plain, but is directly related to another aspect of the conflict. On the one hand, it offers refuge for the birds that inhabit the area ("The old cypress . . . rises up over the walls of the garden, sheltering in its branches all the birds that cross the plain" [122]), but at the same time serves as a constant reminder that Elena is unable to bear children: "The song of the birds that populate the thicket makes [Baltasar] sad. He heard the teacher say one winter that birds are like children, and, ever since that time, when he hears the hubbub overhead, he remembers that

Elena will never be able to have children" (122–23). The accumulation of these images and events in the novel (the drought, the stagnant river, the burning plain, the failure of the crops, the absence of the trees) intensifies the fundamental theme of death and sterility and serves as a backdrop for the existential dilemma of Miguel and Inés.

The Two Protagonists

Although the plight of the two principal characters is exacerbated by life in the small town, their immediate problems originate in the city. Miguel learns of his illness long before visiting the town, and Inés's pregnancy results from her relationship with Agustín in Madrid. Nonetheless, the village and the two central characters are intimately related by the thematic parallel of anguish and death. The life/death contrast of the plain takes form in each of the two protagonists, and is developed following a pattern of existential reciprocity. That is, rather than underscore one particular dimension of the novel, such as character, milieu, or social revelation, Fernández Santos balances these factors so that each gains meaning in conjunction with the other, and is dependent upon the other for the principal shape that it takes. Thus the barren and hostile landscape of the plain merges with the personal conflicts of the characters in order to convey a profound sense of despair and pessimism.

The life/death dimension of the novel is represented from the outset by means of a brief descriptive fragment, separated from the main body of the narrative, that portrays a cemetery on the outskirts of the city. The scene is dominated by the graves of children, and the contrast between life and death, the silence of the cemetery and the noise and activity of the city, provides a thematic synthesis of the work as a whole. The body of the novel then begins with a juxtaposition of the stories of Miguel and Inés in alternating chapters. While Miguel transfers his insane uncle (who later dies) to a new asylum, Inés unsuccessfully attempts to poison herself. As the novel progresses, however, it is Miguel who incarnates most dramatically the life/death theme on both a physical and psychological level.

In the first place, Miguel is burdened by his family's history of disease, and often worries about dying at an early age. Since both of his parents are dead, and his uncle dies in a sanatorium during the course of the novel, Miguel's preoccupation with death and loneliness is rationally motivated. Furthermore, Miguel suffers from the physical pain of tuberculosis and is often debilitated by coughing spells and insomnia. As his sickness progresses he realizes that he has lost control over his body, that the disease dominates his physical movements and restricts the type of life that he is able to lead. Yet the physical pain of his daily life pales when measured against the exis.ential anguish and despair that accompanies it. The fear of death constantly haunts Miguel, yet it is precisely the possibility of death that compels him to examine his life, to reflect on the passing of time, and to identify the meaning that he has forged for himself. What he encounters in his meditations, however, is a vacuous existence in which he feels completely alone and abandoned.

Early in the novel Miguel reflects on his life and affirms that something must give it meaning: "Something must exist, a small conviction, a faith in himself, in the world, so that even without his being aware of it, it would have given some sense to his passage through life, and now to his death" (76). In general, however, Miguel experiences a dissociation of life and meaning and grows aware that his existence is completely devoid of purpose. He wonders if the secret of life lies in its renunciation, but at the same time he explores his past in hope of uncovering a rational design for his existence. Unfortunately, however, "The days that followed his childhood, what good were they? They only brought to mind the images of his uncle Antonio dying slowly in the asylum, the death of his father, loneliness, doubt, a vague attempt to understand the world and, finally, a cortege of hours without meaning, a profound sense of failure" (242). Miguel's preoccupation with both his past and future eventually yields to an acceptance of the abyss between being and meaning. He experiences no sense of accomplishment or fulfillment, and thus his life lacks authenticity. He is plagued by the fear of death and tormented by the belief that he has left nothing behind to verify that he ever existed. At the same time, however, he contemplates the potential liberation from anguish that death may afford him.

Although Miguel's dilemma stems in large part from his physical illness, his existential conflict is clearly aggravated by his stay in the town. Miguel becomes entrapped in the tedium and monotony of daily life in the village, and his thoughts grow more somber as time passes. His flight from Madrid represented a passive abstention from life, and his visit to the town is thematically important to the extent that it reaffirms his meaningless existence. His long walks through the countryside, the hours that he spends reading, and the conversations with Soledad and Inés serve to magnify the emptiness both of Miguel and of the milieu that he has chosen to inhabit. The only element around him that represents an affirmation of life is Inés's desire to give birth to her baby. Everything else (the drought, crop failure, poverty, etc.) serves to intensify Miguel's contradictory wish for both life and death. The semiconscious state of sleep therefore becomes crucial for Miguel, since the feeling of nonexistence associated with it offers temporary escape: "Life, age, time, pain, nothing existed. . . . An emptiness, an infinite nothingness where the breath that animates the heart of man is born. He didn't fear death in those moments, because living and dying were the same thing" (191). By the end of the novel, however, Miguel articulates a death wish, both as a means of avoiding anguish and achieving happiness: "To die young, to die as a child, in the peace of being seven years old. . . . To fade away, falling little by little into a gentle sleep, convinced of the joyful security of waking up one day and finding [his parents] again" (242).

Miguel's ambivalent desire both for life (i.e., meaning) and for death is complemented most directly by his relationship with Inés. Following her unsuccessful suicide attempt and the failure of her relationship with Agustín, Inés returns to her town despite the protest of her sister. Inés's refusal to obtain an abortion serves as a pointed contrast to her earlier wish to take her life, but the return to her village forces her to confront the conflicting forces of the plains. What is important about Inés in relation to Miguel, however, is that she counterbalances within the milieu of the town his profound despair. She has resolved to have her baby and permit the force of life to determine her future: "Inés . . . wondered what life would be like by Miguel's side. She wanted to live. . . . By Miguel's side her serene confidence would return. The child would be born. She didn't want to think of anything else" (170).

Inés and Miguel fall in love (although their feelings are never expressed openly), and they fantasize about living in the company of one another. Miguel imagines himself as the child's father, while Inés looks forward to giving birth. The unborn child thus represents a source of hope and vitality for each of the characters. The timid intimacy of their relationship provides only shortlived happiness, however. Miguel is called to Madrid for the burial of his uncle, and his close contact with death and the vision of his abandoned relative rekindle his own depression. When he returns to the town, he and Inés seem like strangers. Inés ultimately suffers a miscarriage, and the bond between her and Miguel is permanently severed. Inés remains in the town, however, while Miguel returns to Madrid for surgery. Their relationship (i.e., the desire for life) ends abruptly, and each must confront again the conflict between death and life that represents the locus of their anguish and despair.

Social Commentary

The life/death dilemma incarnated by Miguel and Inés also inspires the most explicit social criticism of the novel. The notion of physical illness recurs throughout the narrative and affects rural and urban Spain as well as the upper and lower economic classes. The author's most direct commentary on the problem, however, emerges from the parallel between Miguel and the younger Rojo brother, who suffers from silicosis after working for several years in the local mine. Like Miguel, the young Rojo has difficulty breathing and needs immediate medical care and rest. Unlike Miguel, with his ambivalence in the face of death, Rojo manifests only the spirit of life: "He very much wanted to live, and he actually deserved to be saved, because his love, his desire, was an immense, irrepressible love of life, something that he carried within him" (118). Yet Rojo's medical problem underscores an equally tragic economic one. On the one hand, he cannot afford to enter a hospital because he earns only a small amount of money. On the other, he can no longer work in the mine because he cannot breath the polluted air. Fernández Santos vividly describes the noxious working conditions of the mine: "A fine, milky dust came from the soil, enveloping the boy. Small shiny particles flew in all directions. The white cloud rose little by little, transforming the sweat of his chest into a dirty shirt, forming a grotesque mask around his irritated eyes. Suddenly, the noise of the machine stopped, at the same time that a tearing, convulsive cough burst forth" (107).

When Rojo is forced to leave the mine and is no longer able to earn a living, he and his brother conspire to steal the jewelry of Doña Constanza (a rich widow) in order to pay the medical fees at a private hospital. Although the younger Rojo opposes the plan, the two brothers steal the jewels and flee the town. They are quickly caught by the police, however, and face a sentence of several years in prison. While the sequences depicting the theft and eventual arrest of the two brothers create a certain amount of intrigue in the novel, the incident clearly serves to buttress the author's social concerns. Although disease attacks both the rich and the poor, the capacity to overcome illness is often determined by class distinctions. Miguel's trip to the country merely postpones his surgery. Rojo's poverty, on the other hand, precludes the possibility of surgical cure. Fernández Santos's message here is both clear and compelling, and he permits the younger Rojo brother to articulate it for him: "Before, everyone, rich and poor, died when they were taken ill. Everyone the same, equal, like God wills; but now, Juan, who spent the day reading newspapers from Madrid, had told him that with a lot of money his sickness could be cured; with a lot of money and not working and some injections that recently had been created. The doctor, the husband of the widow, had died of that. If it had happened now, he would have been saved" (174). Poverty is thus linked in the novel to social delinquency as well as to the very essence of life and death.

Fernández Santos also includes in *In the Fire* several characters who enhance his realistic portrayal of provincial life. We are able to observe the frustrations of a sterile wife (Elena) who is obsessed with bearing children; an old man who lives with memories of the Spanish-American War; a wealthy widow who vacillates between devotion to her deceased husband and her sexual entanglements with Zoila, another resident of the town; a young woman who yearns to be married but can find no attractive suitor; a conniving gypsy who is killed by Zoila after he rapes Zoila's daughter. As in *The Untamed*, none of these peripheral figures emerges as a major character, yet each functions to enhance the collective sense of frustration and despair defining the town as a whole. Characters appear and disappear from the narrative at random intervals, and their presence contributes to the realistic slice of life that Fernández Santos aims to represent.

The technical devices of *In the Fire* are for the most part patterned after those employed in *The Untamed*. Character interaction occurs through extensive dialogue, and series of scenes and persons are juxtaposed to provide an overview of daily life. An omniscient narrator records events and offers an objective representation of characters and their actions. But the active intervention of the narrator is increased significantly in *In the Fire* through the rendering of privileged information about the motivations and thoughts of the characters. In *The Untamed*, the narrator infrequently penetrates the consciousness of a character, and for the most part remains in the background as events unfold. In *In the Fire*, however, narrative presence is more immediate, not only because of the expanded descriptive material within the discourse, but also because the narrator probes the thought processes of the characters and reveals their conflicts. A typical example of how this technique functions is found in Miguel's doubts about his journey through Spain: "At that moment [Miguel] was wondering if the trip truly had any purpose. He had decided to take it one night, in the solitude of his room, and now, in the light of the day, he wasn't sure about wanting to continue. Of course, imagining the empty, absurd hours in the boarding house in Madrid helped him decide to continue" (70). Fernández Santos by no means experiments with stream-of-consciousness ramblings, but rather conveys the thoughts of his characters through the conventional use of third-person omniscience and reportage.

The representation of characters' thoughts in *In the Fire* often enables Fernández Santos to depart from the straight chronological flow of the narrative. Since mental processes may project into the future or recall experiences from the distant past, Fernández Santos is able to overcome temporal restrictions simply by following the inclinations of the mind. This is evident, for example, when Miguel's memory is triggered by a photograph from his youth, when he dreams of his father, who died several years before, or when he contemplates the future with Inés. Certainly, the free association of ideas is not a technical innovation for prose narrative in Spain, but for Fernández Santos it represents a modification of the rigid behaviorist technique of *The Untamed* and allows for greater psychological depth in the portrayal of his characters.

Laberintos

Laberintos [Labyrinths] was published in 1964, during a period when Fernández Santos was devoting most of his creative energy to film and television. The book was generally ignored by the reading public and inspired a negative reaction from the critical establishment. Balbino Marcos of *Reseña*, for example, observed that the novel formed part of the social-realistic trend of the Generation of 1950, but lamented that a writer of Fernández Santos's reputation had not produced a work of higher literary quality.[10] J. R. Marra López of *Insula* commented that the novel left him "unsatisfied" and hoped that Fernández Santos would escape the "narrative labyrinth" in which he seemed to be trapped.[11] José Battló, writing in *Cuadernos Hispanoamericanos*, completely dismissed the novel and suggested that it was merely a hollow imitation of novelistic forms that Fernández Santos had helped forge during the 1950s.[12] Although *Labyrinths* is perhaps the least interesting of Fernández Santos's novels, it is by no means totally devoid of literary value. It reaffirms the author's commitment during this period to portraying the ills of contemporary Spanish society, and complements his first two novels in terms of narrative technique and the reiterated thematic preoccupation of abulia and tedium. In contrast to his earlier rural novels, however, the narrative focuses on several mediocre painters and writers of the Madrid café society rather than on the inhabitants of isolated and impoverished villages.

Similar to precedents observed in *The Untamed* and *In the Fire*, there is scant narrative progression in *Labyrinths* that can be described as plot. A

small group of painters and writers from Madrid visits Segovia during
Holy Week, and as the novel develops the characters move about the
city, watch the religious processions, sit and drink in the cafés, and visit
with friends from Segovia. Very little of substance happens in the novel,
and the characters follow the same pattern of inactivity that defines their
life in Madrid. Although Fernández Santos concentrates for the most
part on developing the group as a collective protagonist, he focuses
specific attention on Pedro and Celia, a young couple whose marriage
stands on the verge of complete dissolution. Pedro claims to be a writer,
although he has published only one book in several years and has done
little with his life but participate in *tertulias* and pass time in cafés. Celia
aspires to be a painter, but is oppressed both by the inertia of Pedro and
the few opportunities available to exhibit her works. The two characters
resent each other intensely, and vividly incarnate the tedium of existence
that Fernández Santos aims to convey. Other members of the group
include Julio, an art critic who knows very little about art; Daniel, a
frustrated academic who is forced to give private classes while he awaits a
university position; Pablo, a second-rate painter who has been having an
affair with Celia for nearly two years; and several other marginal characters who participate in conversations and random activities. Viewed as a
whole, the group becomes a caricature of artistic and individual mediocrity, despite the self-important and elitist convictions that characterize
their discussions.

   In addition to the development of a collective protagonist, *Labyrinths*
displays several other similarities with *The Untamed* and *In the Fire*.
Fernández Santos sets the action in a limited physical environment and
creates an accompanying psychological milieu of tedium and abulia.
Physical illness appears again in *Labyrinths*, and the notion of spiritual
poverty and isolation intensifies the emptiness of the characters' daily
existence. For the most part, Fernández Santos again follows the technical constructs of his earlier novels. The objective, third-person narrator
records events without apparent judgment, with the extensive use of
dialogue allowing for the immediate presentation of actions and the
direct portrayal of characters. Apart from broad similarities in tone,
theme, and technique, however, the specific reality represented in
Labyrinths differs markedly from that of *The Untamed* and *In the Fire*. In
the first place, scant space is afforded to the portrayal of the physical
milieu. While the notion of geographic determinism plays an important
role in his first two novels, it is absent from *Labyrinths*. The setting is
portrayed simply as one more element of the narrative rather than as the
dominant influence. The characters do not confront harsh climatic con-

ditions or depend upon the soil for economic sustenance, nor do they suffer the isolation associated with life in a rural village. In this sense, therefore, the physical setting of *Labyrinths* does not influence the existential choices available to the characters or limit their possibilities.

Fernández Santos does not name Segovia as the setting for his novel, but the reader familiar with that provincial capital can easily recognize it from the brief descriptions of the cathedral, streets, and plaza, and from the characters' train ride to the city. Despite the apparent insignificance of the physical environment, however, the choice of Segovia is not a fortuitous one. Fernández Santos spent the Civil War years there as a refugee, and he includes several autobiographical elements in the narrative through the principal character, Pedro. It would be inaccurate to conclude that Pedro is intended to represent Fernández Santos, but the circumstances of his youth frequently run parallel to those of the author's own life. Like Fernández Santos, Pedro was vacationing with his family in the mountains when the war broke out and was evacuated to Segovia by Nationalist troops. Also like the author, Pedro spent long hours in Segovia playing by himself, and recalls watching soldiers march out of the city wearing the Heart of Jesus. Pedro remembers that his father was called upon to serve as a guard in the town prison (as was the father of Fernández Santos), and later reflects on his study of Philosophy and Letters at the University of Madrid, his obsession with literary *tertulias*, and how he left the university in 1950 before finishing his degree—all in a manner similar to Fernández Santos's own life. The three years that Pedro spent in Segovia during the war clearly affect his psychological makeup in the present, and his friends complain that he too frequently tells stories about the war years. This is not to suggest, of course, that *Labyrinths* represents a spiritual catharsis for Fernández Santos, but it does provide insight into the author's recollection of the war and its lingering influence on him.

Problems and Themes

As previously mentioned, Fernández Santos's principal concern in *Labyrinths* centers on the group of painters and writers who meet in Segovia during Holy Week. Each of the characters is afflicted with a personal burden (e.g., Julio's failure as a critic, Daniel's frustrated academic career, Pablo's mediocre painting, Fornell's break with the group), but for the most part the narrative is structured so that the individual event is assimilated into the collective action. Thus the problems of inertia and boredom are represented by a broad range of activities in a variety of circumstances. The notion of "representation" is crucial here, because Fernández Santos does not attempt to use his narrative for probing the psychological complexities of the characters, but rather for rendering objectively and directly the events and dialogue as manifestations of existential dilemmas. The external behavior of the characters thus becomes the focal point for thematic development and provides the impetus for the forward movement of the action.

The principal theme of collective tedium is conveyed from the outset of the novel. The train to Segovia carries people who "were fleeing from the tedium of Madrid"[13] and hoped to find diversion during their few days in Segovia. Soon after their arrival, however, it becomes apparent that the change in location does not alter the daily routine or outlook of the group. Much of the conversation revolves around how to make the afternoon pass quickly, what to do until dinner, how to kill time. Vicente Jordans, an arrogant art dealer who acts as agent for the group, reveals in his eyes "all the tedium in the world" (144), while Julio most succinctly sums up the daily routine of the group when he comments, "I'm getting bored. I'm getting bored like I can't begin to tell you" (43). In short, Fernández Santos achieves thematic intensity by offering the direct statements of the characters, as well as through the observations of the third-person narrator.

The recurrent use of direct representation in order to enhance theme also points to what is perhaps the basic weakness of *Labyrinths*: the failure to examine the motivations or explain the impetus for the characters' abulic existence. Except for his portrayal of Pedro and Celia, Fernández Santos remains content to observe and report external behavior. On the surface, this would seem to resemble the narrative technique of *The Untamed*. But there is a fundamental difference between the two novels that makes the earlier work a more complex and better piece of fiction. In *The Untamed*, as well as in *In the Fire*, Fernández Santos not only represents the profound abulia of provincial life, but also examines the root causes of the problem: geographical determinism, isolation, poverty, illness, drought. In *Labyrinths*, however, he focuses on the symptoms of the malady without offering insight into the source or cause. He is not concerned with the sequence of motive, act, and consequence, but simply with the act, with the present state of things. Clearly, the novel portrays the failure of the characters to achieve a vital professional or personal existence. Without background information about the characters, however, and without the deterministic impact of the physical setting, the narrative becomes a series of scenes that represent again and again the mediocrity of individuals who are essentially uninteresting people with little of value to do or to say. The reader senses this at the beginning of the novel, but never discovers what it is about the characters (or society) that determines their vacuous existence.

On occasion the members of the group discuss art and literature, revealing a superficial knowledge of the artistic tendencies of the time. The group itself, dubbed "Grupo 60," is regarded by art critics as an abnormal, even "sickly" collection of young painters who have little to offer the art world. Nonetheless, they have achieved a certain amount of success, primarily due to the hard work of Fornell, who "gave [the group] form and cohesion while struggling with the abulia of the others" (121–22). The young painters reject the representational art of the social realists, but their own aesthetic doctrine remains vague except for the belief that "the anguish of the present world is reflected in their painting" (28). Their discussions of art and literature (e.g., Pedro's condemnation of Hemingway; Social Realism) never reach the level of intellectual debate, since they are vitiated by the same lack of enthusiasm, personal conflicts, and cynicism characterizing other aspects of their lives. The characters quickly grow bored with serious discussion, since their real interest in art is rooted in the desire for material gain and personal recognition. This again points to a fundamental difference between Fernández Santos's first two novels and *Labyrinths*. In the earlier works, the characters do not resort to intellectual masks or pretentious subterfuges that permit them to circumvent their emptiness, but accept their destiny and suffer the consequences of their inactivity. In *Labyrinths*, the characters are also vividly aware of their meaningless existence, yet they attempt to finesse their way through life by giving the appearance of artistic and intellectual commitment. In reality, of course, they suffer from the same inertia as the characters of *The Untamed* and *In the Fire*, and are consumed by a monotonous existence that promises no opportunity for escape.

The most cynical commentary on the group stems from Julio's work on a pamphlet about Fornell. Founder of the Grupo 60 and once its most important member, Fornell has now fallen out of favor with the group's agent. Thus his painting will no longer receive favorable publicity and preferential treatment at exhibits. Fornell's demotion in status means that Julio's nearly completed study may no longer be of interest, and Julio fears that he will have to abandon the project. Yet Celia suggests that his study will still be valuable: "That's not a problem. . . . You simply change the name and make it about someone else, about Fontán himself . . . what difference does it make? You just talk about cosmic spaces, or say that it's very Spanish, that it has a lot of strength. Everyone

likes that" (129). After pondering Celia's suggestion, Julio agrees that it
is a good one: "Celia was right. What difference did it make if it was
Fornell or Fontán?" (130). The general idea expressed here, of course, is
that art criticism consists of well-written, but meaningless, clichés. The
immediate object of attention, however, is Julio's willingness to prosti-
tute the legitimate intellectual value of critical work in favor of material
gain: "The work of the critic wasn't a bad game if you knew how to play
it, providing that nothing too much was risked. Later would come the
art books and then the lectures throughout America. There was money
to earn there and a bit of fame, too" (130).

Principal Characters

Pedro and Celia do not form part of the Grupo 60, but their activities
are closely tied to the group and to the café *tertulias*. The pervasive
malaise of the circle of friends is represented more poignantly by Pedro
and Celia since, in contrast to the other characters, the narrative explains
the causes of their discontent and the history of their existential predicament. For the most part, Fernández Santos is concerned in *Labyrinths*
with time as a day-to-day continuum, as a small-scale reflection of the
human condition. In his portrayal of Pedro (and to a lesser degree of
Celia), however, he employs techniques of multiple temporal inter-
penetration, such as flashback and memory, demonstrating the cumulative
effects of time. In his previous novels, the sense of temporal duration is
conveyed by the use of specific images: the still hands of a clock, the
appearance of an old tree, or the ruins of a church all suggest that time
weighs heavily upon the characters. In *Labyrinths*, however, Fernández
Santos seeks to illustrate how the present is determined to a large degree
by past events, relationships, and dilemmas. Thus Pedro's life in Segovia
during the Civil War and his subsequent failures at the University
of Madrid and in Paris become critical to the understanding of his
character.

The narrator explains, for example, that for much of his childhood
Pedro remained aloof from his family: "His mother said he was a
pampered child. His uncle, that he was pampered and a little capricious.
His absent air, his eagerness to wander alone, bothered them. He always
seemed far away from them. That prolonged solitude had pursued him
throughout his life" (131). Pedro's loneliness does not abate following
his marriage to Celia and continues to torment him. His solitude and
isolation are in fact intensified by his relationship with Celia. Despite
the physical intimacy of their first years of marriage, Pedro cannot escape

the feeling that "his relationship with her [was] distant, artificial" (132). Their remoteness from one another is exacerbated, ironically, by their frequent conversations. For the most part, dialogue between them consists either of bitter reproaches or banal platitudes that essentially preclude the possibility of intimate communication. As do their friends, Pedro and Celia remain indifferent to each other's emotional needs. Hence their marriage is characterized by an immutable polarity that magnifies the tedium and emptiness of their daily life.

Fernández Santos interpolates a flashback sequence that portrays Pedro and Celia's stay in Paris during the early years of their marriage. Pedro's desire to develop his talents in a more creative atmosphere and the need to escape their life in Madrid lead the couple to spend a year in Paris among the artistic and intellectual crowd. The act of leaving Madrid is significant, since it represents potential liberation from the sterility of their previous life-style. Yet their effort fails miserably, because they follow a pattern of life in Paris (*tertulias*, idleness, boredom) that parallels and repeats their existence in Spain. Despite their inactivity, however, Pedro clings to the belief that conditions will improve and that he and Celia will be able to enter the mainstream of intellectual life. They eventually return to Spain, of course, and the erstwhile experience in Paris becomes a precursor to Pedro's later failures. After his return to Madrid Pedro's future ceases to exist in a positive sense, since it consists only of repeating the frustrations of the past. He is haunted by the "aspect of abulic defeat" (45) of Paris, and is unable to realize his life in either a professional or broadly existential fashion. Fernández Santos by no means suggests that Pedro has become psychologically unbalanced but simply that he is debilitated by failure and despair. As a result, he not only makes of himself, but of Celia as well, a victim of his inertia.

Pedro places part of the blame for his failure on his uncle, who refused to help Pedro during the early years of his writing. Pedro's uncle, a well-known author during the 1930s, has written little in several years and now lives with memories of past success. He frequently meets with other artists and actors of his generation, and Pedro is repelled by their pretentious condemnation of today's youth when they, in Pedro's view, have become the embodiment of inactivity and decadence. Pedro reproaches them not only for their pompous life-style, but for their material greed and intellectual dishonesty. They discuss Spanish art without having ever visited the Prado, and presume to be cultured, although they have never attended the opera or a concert. Pedro's condemnation of his uncle creates the most poignant irony of the novel. Pedro and his friends reveal the same vanity and greed that characterize the older generation, having fallen into a similar state of lethargy. The tragedy of their situation is that Pedro's group of friends has grown bored with life before having achieved anything at all.

Celia's character is not as well defined as Pedro's, and the motivations for her actions are less evident. As the novel progresses, however, it becomes clear that Celia refuses to conform to the cycle of inactivity and that she seeks to assert her will despite the oppressive influence of Pedro and his friends. Throughout the years of her marriage Celia has attempted to conciliate the conflicting elements of their existence: she has acted to affirm her independence while struggling to maintain her relationship with Pedro. She has continued to paint (in contrast to Pedro, who no longer writes), and has pursued a love affair with Pablo that is tacitly accepted by Pedro's silence. When a friend suggests that she may be able to work in Italy, she vows to take the job even if Pedro refuses to go along. Yet as time passes, Celia grows aware that, despite consistent efforts to vitalize her existence, the oppressive milieu that surrounds her is slowly eroding her self-determination, and that her future has gradually come to coincide with Pedro's. When her affair with Pablo no longer offers an escape from her tedious life, she finally realizes that it is necessary "to put an end to the inertia of the last few years, to what was only a sad imitation of life" (112).

Following a series of disputes with Pedro in Segovia, Celia resolves to abandon her husband and return to Madrid. Her decision to leave Pedro, however, is less significant than the psychological and existential change that accompanies it. She experiences "a new feeling of freedom [being] born in her. For the first time she also understood that her life was about to change. Her days with Pedro, like that week, like her love for Pablo, had ended" (203). Even Pedro comes to realize that "the destiny of his wife depended only on her" (205). Celia thus dissociates herself from the chain of being of her immediate past (i.e., she rejects Pedro, Pablo, the group, etc.), and therefore automatically places on herself full responsibility for shaping meaning in the world. Her desire for self-realization represents the only assertive act in the novel and constitutes a marked contrast with the abulia and routine that she has left behind.

Labyrinths is much less a social novel than *The Untamed* and *In the Fire*, since Fernández Santos does not examine in it the problems of poverty and social injustice that form integral parts of his earlier works. Although Pedro and Celia exist on a meager income, while Joaquín lives comfortably as part of the Segovian upper class, there is no attempt in the novel to criticize social and economic inequality. Despite the diminished social concern, however, *Labyrinths* owes much to the author's first two novels in technical construction and character development. Dialogue is utilized to represent directly the sterility of personal interaction and to demonstrate the atrophied existence of the characters. As in *The Untamed* and *In the Fire*, the development of a collective protagonist in *Labyrinths* implies that existential emptiness is not merely the dilemma of one or two individuals, but rather characterizes an entire group or generation of persons. Fernández Santos's preoccupation with this theme in each of his first three novels suggests that he views inertia and abulia not only as a problem identified with certain social classes or the inhabitants of specific geographic locations but also as a malady deeply rooted in the Spanish psyche during the postwar years. As he illustrates in *The Untamed*, "character is destiny," and the destiny of the Spanish people in Fernández Santos's early novels is not an optimistic one. *Labyrinths* forms an integral part of this vision, and closes the cycle of objective realism that comprises the author's narrative during the 1950s and early 1960s.

Chapter Three
Existential Despair and the Individual

El hombre de los santos

The eventual recognition of *The Untamed* as one of the major novels of postwar Social Realism placed Fernández Santos in a prominent position among young Spanish writers. He was no longer obliged to struggle to have his work published, and critics devoted ample coverage to his next two novels, *In the Fire* and *Labyrinths*. The mixed reviews accorded the former work, however, and the negative reaction to the latter, created a degree of skepticism concerning Fernández Santos's capabilities as a novelist. Thus the publication of *El hombre de los santos* [The Man of the Saints] in 1969 proved decisive in reestablishing his reputation as one of the most talented writers of the postwar period. The novel was awarded the important Critics' Prize over such formidable competition as Mario Vargas Llosa's *Conversación en la catedral*, Camilo José Cela's *San Camilo, 1936*, and Miguel Delibes's *Parábola del náufrago*, all of which are now recognized as major contributions to contemporary Hispanic narrative. Furthermore, critics lauded *The Man of the Saints* as one of the finest novels of the postwar period. Santiago García Díez, for example, wrote that "It is a novel, like *The Untamed*, that must be considered among the best of our time,"[1] while José Domingo proclaimed in *Insula* that "[The Man of the Saints] returns Fernández Santos to the forefront of our literary activity."[2] Carmen Martín Gaite, an important novelist in her own right, titled her review "Fernández Santos Returns," and concluded that the principal character of the novel "is one of the most serious figures to appear in postwar narrative, and through him the author of *The Untamed* returns to literature through the front door."[3]

The Man of the Saints is much more complex than Fernández Santos's previous novels, but it represents less a break with his social realistic fiction than the emergence of a more mature writer intent on refashioning his techniques and themes. This evolution toward a more innovative brand of narrative is manifest in several important aspects of *The Man of the Saints*. For example, rather than develop a collective protagonist as in his first three novels, Fernández Santos probes the consciousness of a single character, utilizing psychological revelation as his principal narrative tool. The physical milieu of the novel, set in Madrid and several small provincial villages, no longer functions as an element of geographic determinism, but rather serves to complement and intensify the principal theme of isolation and solitude (both physical and spiritual) that is embodied by the protagonist. Fernández Santos also incorporates into the novel several narrative techniques characteristic of the growing body of experimental fiction written in Spain during the late 1960s (e.g., multiple points of view, temporal fragmentation, interior monologue). In addition, his style of writing in *The Man of the Saints* creates a more fluid discourse than that of his earlier works and calls attention to itself as a unique aesthetic element of the narrative. Yet Fernández Santos by no means seeks to invent a self-referential text that is cut off from external social reality. On the contrary, many dialogues and descriptive fragments of the novel evoke the *costumbrista* vision of his social fiction. Likewise, the thematic focus can be traced in part to his earlier novels. Fernández Santos admitted shortly after the publication of *The Man of the Saints* that "I'm a bit weary of being only the author of the *The Untamed.*"[4] At the same time, though, he does not wish to reject outright his past fiction, but rather diversify his ideas and recast his narrative design.

The principal character of *The Man of the Saints*, Antonio Salazar (i.e., "the man of the saints"), works at removing frescoes from old churches and monasteries. He spends several months each year away from his home in Madrid and has gradually grown distant from his wife and daughter. The narrative present of the novel portrays Antonio at work in small villages (Chapters 1 and 4) or at home in Madrid during the wedding of his daughter (Chapters 2 and 3). The final chapter presents Antonio's return to Madrid after a fire prevents him from completing his work at a convent. Although the chronological duration of the novel is approximately one year, the psychological time spans nearly four decades, from Antonio's youth before the Civil War to an unspecified present during the 1960s. Through the memory of Antonio and several other characters, the novelist probes the past, offering a complex portrait of the isolation and despair of life both during and following the Civil War.

Antonio, a former artist, turned to restoration and preservation of art works following the war. His story, however, is not that of an artist who has failed in his profession, but rather of a man who has failed in life. That Antonio was at one time a promising young artist is not important, just as it does not matter that he has earned a comfortable living preserving frescoes. What is important about Antonio, and what lies at the heart of the novel, is the pervasive notion that he has been defeated by life itself. He leads a meaningless and empty existence because he has remained passive in the face of his existential responsibility. This spiritual vacuum plagues every aspect of his existence, but is most dramatically embodied in his work and in his relationships with other persons (in particular his family). Antonio consistently resists communication with others, which eventually causes his complete solitude and impels a course in life that leads to existential nothingness.

In contrast to the characters of *The Untamed* and *In the Fire*, who are oppressed by a deterministic milieu, Antonio is free to make choices that will shape the direction of his life. Yet in both his work and his marriage he has avoided decision and permitted his choices to be appropriated by others, as is especially evident in his professional activities. After ignoring the wishes of his father to pursue a career outside of art (i.e., after making the only assertive decision of his life), Antonio begins to make copies of famous paintings at the Prado shortly after the war. Although economic necessity influenced his decision, Antonio's work at the museum and his later employment by a wealthy patron in Toledo represent more of an abdication of choice than an active assertion of his will. He realized that his copies were "something without value, not even a portrait, that is: nothing, less than nothing,"[5] and even accepted that his life was molded more by external factors than by his own desire to pursue a particular goal: "As always happened with him, the most absurd factors ended up determining the crucial moments of his life" (81).

After growing tired of his work in Toledo, Antonio secured his first job removing frescoes through the intervention of his father-in-law, and has continued to work at the profession for more than two decades. What is ironic here, and what creates and sustains much of Antonio's existential emptiness, is the fact that Antonio believes neither in the intrinsic merit of his work nor in its importance to society. He has spent much of his adult life at a task that is "useless, silly, empty" (216), yet he refuses to explore alternative forms of employment. He is resigned both to the nature of his vocation and to its lack of consequence in the world: "Perhaps all the years kneeling down on the floor, climbing the scaffolds, struggling with the Church Foundation, with priests, mayors, and nuns, meant very little. Perhaps his was not an authentic job, but rather a game. A tiresome game, sometimes hard and always lonely" (38).

Since Antonio consistently doubts the value of his work, and even views it as an officially sanctioned rape of the only thing of value left in many small towns, the reasons for his professional commitment must lie outside the specific nature of his craft. Indeed, as his life progresses the motivation for Antonio stems precisely from the sense of isolation that his work affords him. Rather than attempt to avoid solitude, Antonio actively seeks it out.[6] He could easily do restoration work in Madrid, but prefers instead to live at home for only a few months a year. This is not merely because of the indifference that he feels toward his wife, but also because the solitude of his work enables him to evade the commitments of personal interaction. Antonio at no time seeks to vitalize his life, nor does he attempt to resist the abulia and inertia that weigh upon him. As he travels about Spain he encounters other persons who lead a lonely existence similar to his own (e.g., priests, nuns, a fisherman, old women). All of these figures, although mentioned only briefly, serve to enhance the thematic base of the novel by complementing and amplifying the interfusion of existential anguish and solitude.

Through Antonio, Fernández Santos conveys a sense of the political atmosphere in Spain following the Civil War. Although the protagonist does not explicitly symbolize the Spanish middle class, he nonetheless embodies certain characteristics representative of the conformist mentality of postwar society. For example, he neither knows what is taking place around him nor cares to find out. When stopped by a guerrilla in a small town where he is working and asked if he has heard of the guerrilla resistance, he responds, "No. I rarely go out" (115). When an elderly village doctor questions him about the student uprisings at the university, the protests staged by young priests, or the future role of the Church in Spain, Antonio responds, "I don't know. To tell you the truth, I don't read the newspapers. . . . In Madrid, I rarely go out . . . I don't know. It's difficult to know" (230). In fact, as José Domingo has observed, none of the characters (from the lower or middle classes) demonstrates a concern for the social reality of the country.[7] This absence (or fear) of social and political awareness can be detected in the banal and innocuous conversations carried on in bars and cafés, and is articulated most succinctly when the doctor remarks to Antonio, "I have a feeling that you never admit what you are thinking" (234–35).

Antonio's marriage to Carmen in many ways mirrors the passive acceptance of his professional existence. Characterized by the same sense of inertia, it produces a profound solitude rather than shared intimacy. Antonio is first attracted to Carmen during the war. The human warmth of her family's apartment offers refuge from both the loneliness of his own home and the routine of army life. He finally resolves to marry her following her compassionate understanding of his fear of being sent to the front lines. As time passes, however (and Antonio avoids combat duty), the affection that once existed in their relationship yields to indifference and boredom. Antonio concludes that their wedding should be postponed, but lacks the strength to tell her of his decision. Eventually the two grow completely apart and Antonio realizes in the present that "after so many years, he knows her less now than then, even before they were engaged, down in the basement, during the bombing" (144). This profound estrangement in his marriage further reflects the emptiness of every facet of his life and appears particularly striking when viewed in relation to the broader frame of reference of his past and present: "His mother turned and looked at him. And she wasn't crying. It was an empty face like always. Neither the shadow of his father, nor he himself, nor a vague flash of happiness, nor the pain of the war could be seen in her eyes. It was an empty face and nothing else . . . similar to many others, to Carmen later on; perhaps to his own now" (261).

Time and Memory

As suggested earlier, the repeated commingling of time periods in *The Man of the Saints* represents an important modification of Fernández Santos's technique. Rather than attempt to provide a specific "slice of life" (as in his previous novels), with its limited spatial and temporal purview, Fernández Santos seeks to portray life in all its psychological complexity by making the past an integral part of the present. That is, the past is not structured chronologically and the present does not appear as an isolated instant in time. Instead, the view of the past follows certain impulses and emotions of the characters and emerges as a result of the free association of ideas. By using the time-shift technique, in which the temporal focus continually changes, Fernández Santos gives immediacy to the past so that it is felt to be permeating the present as an essential component of characterization. The narrator in fact suggests the temporal structuring of the novel when Antonio returns to his room one evening: "And once again the walls begin to disappear, to mark the beginning of another night that he doesn't know how long will last, a moment, a year or an entire life of oscillation and memory" (57). It must be pointed out, however, that Fernández Santos does not move his narrative back and forth in time in order to create temporal confusion, as do many contemporary novelists. Instead, he offers specific points of reference in the past (the Civil War) and present (Antonio's work, the wedding) so that a sense of chronological coherence is maintained even though the events portrayed conform to the unordered patterns of memory.

Despite the continual fusion of temporal planes, Antonio often resists the impulses of his memory. This denial of the past shapes Antonio's character in the present and limits the possibility for a meaningful future. First of all, it suggests that very little from his previous life can be remembered in a positive sense. Indeed, the past rarely serves as a source of meaning for Antonio, or even as a refuge from the solitude of the present. Thus when certain memories of the war or of his family begin to appear in his consciousness, Antonio rejects them, for they serve to illuminate the triviality of his life: "And Antonio sees, floating in the shadows, that memory of before, that threshold beyond which he cannot pass, behind which there is nothing, behind which there is only a vast and melancholy emptiness" (192).

Since Antonio's past consists of a series of painful and vacuous experiences, and since he fails to pursue a specific goal in the present, he possesses nothing with which to vitalize his future. As Sartre has written, "Man is nothing else but what he purposes, he exists only in so far as he realizes himself, he is therefore nothing else but the sum of his actions."[8] Antonio desperately needs to escape "the sum of his actions" because they have consistently been passive responses to the world rather than willed choices and assertive acts. His life becomes only a "could-have-been," because he never challenges the world to make it conform to his own vision. This is true of his aspirations to be a painter (125) as well as of his decision to marry Carmen when in fact he was in love with his cousin Tere.

The only positive memory that Antonio consistently evokes centers on his relationship with Tere during and shortly following the Civil War. More than a memory, however, Tere functions as a persistent fantasy that sustains Antonio over the years. In the first place, it is suggested that she and her mother served as mistresses to high-ranking officials of the Republican Army. Thus when Antonio is drafted he asks Tere for help in securing him a safe position in Madrid. As time passes Antonio grows more attracted to her, and his visits to her apartment offer an escape from the war. Although Antonio marries Carmen shortly after the conflict, it is Tere who remains in his thoughts. He can imagine living "with another profession, even without the war, but not without her, a large part of his memories" (283). Only Antonio himself knows "how much of him consists of those memories, of those moments, of that same desire" (284). Like everything else, however, Tere forms part of what he could have made of the present had he been able, as Sartre writes, "to draw his own portrait" in the past. When he finally decides (in the present) to pursue Tere, and proposes to her that they run away together, she gently rejects him. Thus the only possible liberation for Antonio from the solitude of his existence, the single aspect of his past that could have engendered a meaningful future, becomes instead another element of his existential despair.

Antonio's recollections of Tere also inspire memories of the Civil War. In Fernández Santos's first two novels the war is important to the extent that its social and economic aftermath contributes to the decay of rural villages. In *Labyrinths*, the war appears in the memories of a character who experienced the fighting as a child; hence the immediacy of its horror is mitigated by the childhood perspective. In *The Man of the Saints*, however, the Civil War is portrayed as a devastating psychological and physical conflict that created fear, hunger, and isolation in those who were compelled to endure it. Fernández Santos does not explore the opposing political ideologies of the Republican and Nationalist forces, nor does he portray the war as a noble struggle contested by courageous soldiers. Instead, he focuses on psychological stress and fear and the debasement of human values.

Antonio aims only to survive the war, relying upon the implied prostitution of his cousin to avoid the front lines. He is stationed at an air base outside Madrid, where he works as an assistant in the leather shop. Although the base is frequently bombed, and he witnesses and experiences the fear of death, Antonio for the most part remains sheltered from the fighting. Nonetheless, Fernández Santos expresses the brutality and horror of the war and portrays Antonio's fellow soldiers as pathetic figures who have forfeited their sense of humanity. This is evident, for example, when a German plane crashes near their base outside Madrid. Rather than rush to the aircraft in search of survivors, the men become vicious scavengers in pursuit of booty: "Sánchez grabbed with one hand what was still left of the leg, and with the other he pulled on the heel. Antonio saw him leave the nude leg standing upright in the air and then throw it into the gully. . . . Others gathered up a watch, another took a jacket, and Pepe, the electrician, found a Luger. . . . Happy and bloody, they ran from one side of the wreck to the other"(134).

Although the war directly influenced the lives of the soldiers, Fernández Santos shows that it profoundly affected the civilian population as well. The constant bombing of Madrid created a new cultural life in the bomb shelters of the city. At first, the shelters spawned intimacy and shared grief among the people. Later, however, this intimacy turns into "hatred, fear and that wretched feeling of impotence. The sad remoteness and solitude return, and as the days pass, the hunger, fear, and passion are no longer new, and the people down in the basements lead their life isolated from others, like at home" (144—45). The war also created a sense of contingency in the plans and desires of the people, with everything conditioned by the uncertainty of the fighting and the instability of daily existence. As the narrator explains, "Plans and decisions, even an important thing like an engagement—it was customary then to postpone it, make it dependent upon the unforeseeable end of the war" (221). In sum, the war stands as a dramatic point of reference for Antonio's memories, which consistently revolve around the fear and suffering produced by the conflict. The time period of the war (1936—1939) provides a specific point of reference in the past, enabling the reader to distinguish more clearly the evolution of Antonio's loneliness from the prewar days of his youth to his marriage and professional activities after the war came to an end.

Solitude and Emptiness

Two characters who did not experience the war directly, but who serve to reinforce the notion of solitude and emptiness, are Antonio's daughter, Anita, and a young priest who lives in a small mountain village. Like her father, Anita once studied painting, but abandoned art, first to study languages and then to work in an advertising firm. As does her father, Anita lives a hollow existence, underscored—ironically—by her wedding. Although about to be married to Gonzalo (a travel agent), she has carried on a love affair with her married boss. The novelist does not suggest that the affair is illicit or even immoral, but rather shows how it symbolizes the insipid nature of Anita's existence. She has no passion for life, no meaningful vision of what she desires. Like her father, she will marry someone to whom she is not emotionally committed, yet she refuses to delay or cancel the wedding: "But it's necessary to go on, to continue; to go backward now, to delay it, is impossible, prohibited, nobody does it and besides, everyone knows that everything usually works out well, and if it doesn't, you end up getting used to it" (129). Clearly, Anita condemns herself to a life of conjugal indifference by the passive acceptance of circumstances that she is free to alter. Like her father, she refuses to confront her existential responsibility, resolving to grow accustomed to life as it is rather than shape it according to her own particular needs.

While Anita further exemplifies the emptiness of Antonio's family life, the young priest intensifies the theme of solitude to a degree approaching pathological deviance. In many ways, however, his life parallels Antonio's. He endured a childhood of loneliness and isolation with little contact with his parents. Also—as did Antonio—he resisted the career suggestions of his father by studying to become a priest. His days at the seminary were made tolerable only by his attachment to one of the other students, who likewise spent each Sunday without a visit from his parents. Through the memories of the priest and the observations of the third-person narrator, we learn of the friendship between the two students until the friend is killed in a motorcycle accident.

In the narrative present (i.e., the small village where Antonio is removing frescoes), the priest continues to isolate himself from others. Like Antonio, he ponders an escape from his life when it becomes unbearably empty. In contrast to Antonio, however, he is unable to dilute his solitude by moving back and forth between his work and his home. He is haunted by a pervasive emptiness that gradually evolves into a form of psychological aberration. After being humiliated by the visit of his parents to his small town (the first time they had seen him there), he walks through the forest, where he hears the voice and sees the vague shadow of his friend. Although this is the final scene in which the priest appears, we later discover that he has been placed in an asylum for the mentally ill. When the Secretary at the Ministry (Antonio's boss) asks if Antonio had noticed a strangeness about the priest, Antonio responds, "I don't know what I was going to notice. I do remember that he was always by himself" (279). The Secretary's reply, intended to be humorous, is nonetheless a poignant reminder of Antonio's own situation: "What you don't need is to end up like him; remember that you too are always alone" (279). Fernández Santos does not imply here that Antonio will inevitably lose his grip on reality. Indeed, the protagonist is fully aware of his dilemma and consciously preserves his lonely existence. Although the pursuit of solitude is not in itself a cause of psychological illness, Fernández Santos clearly suggests that it almost inevitably results in anguish and despair.

Several other events and characters also enhance the principal theme of solitude. The most vivid instance centers on a community of nuns for whom Antonio is removing recently discovered frescoes. Although the narrative offers only a brief glimpse into their lives, several nuns emerge with individual identities. The elderly Sister Teresa, for example, is sustained less by the spiritual comfort of the present than by memories of her youth. Her life at the convent has forced her to sever physical ties with the past (e.g., "the sights of Madrid, the avenues of Paris and Barcelona, and above all of Havana . . ." [207]), but she repeatedly evokes her earlier life by searching through an old box filled with photographs. This constant recollection of the past not only represents an escape from old age, but also a return to a time when she lived within the world rather than isolated from it. Similarly, the abbess often recalls the blurred faces of her family, and their psychological presence represents a marked contrast with the "empty church, the immense, always-empty choir" (241—42). The assistant superior is likewise plagued by the fear of loneliness ("I find myself so alone here sometimes" [226]), and prays that she will not be separated from her close friend Sister Aurea. The novelist does not seek to criticize religious life by portraying the nuns' lonely existence, but simply suggests that solitude in some form afflicts all human beings, even those with a profound and sincere spiritual faith.

One of the most important symbols of solitude in the novel is the wall that separates Antonio's house from a nearby park. During construction of the house shortly after the war the wall restricted an area still covered by land mines. As time passed, however, the wall remained intact, gradually coming to symbolize Antonio's isolation from the world around him. This is explicitly verified at the end of the novel when the wall is finally destroyed. Antonio has returned from an outing with Tere, resolved to forge a new life with her. She rejects him, but the significance of his effort to commune with the world is affirmed by the demolition of the wall: "Never before seeing the pine trees, the black evergreen oaks, the tobacco-colored stain of the [other] oak trees, would he have believed that the wall separated so much, that it hid so much, that it was so massive, so tall. Seeing now the waves of hills, each one blending into another, dominating that imprecise line of the horizon, it seems incredible that all of it had been there, so near, for so many years"(288). At the same time, however, the final scene underscores Antonio's intense suffering and reveals that he is aware of his place in the world: "Almost in the center of the great, still darkness [of the night] there is a tiny glow that grows bright from time to time. It must be the glow of a cigarette. . . . Now that there is no traffic, and the distant roar of trains is not heard, the only thing that gives life to the park is the chirping of crickets and the glow of the cigarette. That life of darkness is [Antonio's] life, and his solitary existence will last as long as the still glow that grows bright from time to time" (288). Antonio plainly demonstrates here that he perceives his insignificance as an individual and that his life is devoid of essence. His is an empty existence, ephemeral like the burning of a cigarette, never to be vitalized.

Fernández Santos's view of the isolation and ruin of small provincial towns, which forms an important part of *The Untamed* and *In the Fire*, also appears as a correlative thematic concern in *The Man of the Saints*. Most of the villages where Antonio works languish in poverty and show few signs of life. The hamlet near the French border, for example, is "semiempty now and almost always" (9), while during the winter it will be "asleep, deserted, with no other sign of life than the sound of avalanches and snow storms" (35–36). Like most buildings in moribund villages, the church is "a large old cave, abandoned and dirty" (72). As in his earlier novels, Fernández Santos offers insight into certain aspects of daily life in the towns. We learn, for example, how the existence of one or two television sets draws persons of the community closer together, how adultery is arbitrated by the awarding of sheep to the offended husband, and how revenge is taken for the sake of family pride. This same kind of *costumbrista* narration characterizes certain scenes in Madrid, especially those that portray events during the wedding and discussions at Modesto's bar. As Spanish critic Jorge Rodríguez Padrón has observed, "Dialogues, scenes, objects, and persons form a diversified whole that gives the novel a very Spanish tone."[9] Thus Fernández Santos does not completely abandon the elements of his previous narrative, but integrates them with innovative features of his style and technique to enhance the psychological revelation of individuals.

Style and Technique

In his first three novels Fernández Santos generally adhered to the Neo-realistic view that style and technique primarily involve choosing the most efficient and effective words to express best the subject at hand. Although occasionally employing a highly metaphorical descriptive fragment, he offered for the most part an objective portrayal of reality characterized by straightforward narration and authentic dialogue. In *The Man of the Saints*, however, both style and technique are foregrounded to form an important aspect of Fernández Santos's emerging new narrative. Dialogue is still authentic, and the portrayal of external reality remains an integral part of authorial intent. But the stylistic and technical elements of the novel call attention to themselves and enhance the aesthetic and purely literary qualities of the work.

In addition to the fragmentation of time discussed earlier, the novelist experiments with multiple narrative points of view. For example, we learn from three sources (the third-person narrator, Antonio, the reflections of the priest) that the priest endures a lonely existence. On occasion the narrative switches to the first person (e.g., with the abbess and assistant superior), and at times a flashback occurs within a flashback (e.g, pp. 58−62). The wedding of Anita is conveyed through the consciousness of Antonio, Anita's lover, and the third-person narrator. Antonio bids farewell to Anita through a form of interior monologue in Chapter 1, Anita offers a similar interior monologue when she says good-bye to her father in Chapter 2, and her lover repeats the same pattern in his own monologue following the wedding. In addition to the stylistic parallels of each of these segments, the themes of melancholy and isolation are also enhanced. It is significant that the farewells are voiced silently, demonstrating the fear and inability of the characters to communicate with persons to whom they are intimately linked by family or sexual ties. The overall accumulation of these diverse technical constructs, coupled with the movement back and forth in time, creates a complex reality, multifaceted in its perspective and profound in its psychological revelation.

Several stylistic elements also suggest a movement away from the norms of Neo-realism. The self-effacing prose of Fernández Santos's earlier works yields to a more complex and at times poetic discourse. The most common stylistic trait of the novel is the amassing of nouns, verbs, and adjectives into groups of three. This compounding occurs most frequently with adjectives and enables Fernández Santos to suggest fine nuances of meaning or emphasize a particular description or event. For example, the sky is portrayed as "blue, terse, brilliant" (23), and German planes are "silvery, monotonous, boring" (130). In the first instance, the sky is depicted by two "objective" adjectives (blue, brilliant) and one emotive description (terse). Thus the sky becomes a concise symbol of both the meteorological circumstances and psychological condition of the moment. In the second example, the airplanes seem to be pieces of silver, but are also boring and monotonous, which suggests that they appear frequently and interrupt daily activities. Other groups of three adjectives convey a completely emotive image. For example, the world is "so sad, so insipid and boring" (256), or the voice of a bartender is "sour, hard, tired" (184). Sister Aurea is depicted as "scarcely happy, so sad and silent" (251), while a young boy helping Antonio is "so cute, so obliging, so nice" (255). The adjectives used in these sequences (and in several others) convey different shades of meaning and give depth and multiformity to the object being described.

Fernández Santos occasionally groups series of adjectives and verbs together to enhance a particular situation, as, for example, when Antonio evokes the memory of Tere's apartment. He recalls the frustrations of their relationship as "that which one cannot eat, nor drink, nor destroy, and which remains intact, invincible, eternal" (193). Descriptive fragments are intensified by the use of four or more adjectives or verbs in a series. The portraits from Tere's apartment are "sold, dead, forgotten, lost" (271); the windows in her stairwell reveal "gray, sour, penetrating emptiness, stale with the moldy sediment of shaken rugs, oil from the furnace, nap, dust, and smoke" (272); Antonio's activities during the war consist of having to "get up each morning, go down into the shelter, be afraid, suffer, get mad, fight with Máximo, admire him, hate him, go out, dig, go to the latrine, desire his cousin . . ." (164). This build-up of adjectives and verbs provides a rhythmic effluence to Fernández Santos's style, enabling him to achieve a completeness of expression that differs radically from the elliptic narrative of his earlier novels.

A wide range of other stylistic devices enhances the overall aesthetic quality of the discourse. Fernández Santos makes frequent use of anaphora to add rhythm and length to a description (e.g., pp. 48, 54, 179, 181, 236, etc.) and uses parallelism throughout his narrative with similar results. In several descriptive passages he utilizes personification, thereby enhancing the poetic essence of the object or scene described. This can be seen, for example, in the opening passages of the novel in which the river "lies asleep in the forest of chestnut trees" (7); the "lazy columns of smoke" (7) rise out of the chimneys, and the two churches of the town "look at one another in silence" (9). Fernández Santos even employs several surrealistic images to enhance the ethereal nature of certain incidents. The church is seen "floating immobile" (18) in the middle of the plaza; the "silence of men and animals floated on the mountain" (24); Antonio's memory "floated in the shadows" (192). When Anita and her boss make love in the latter's car, "The interior of the car was erased, it floated, fell softly who knows where, without touching the bottom, and their legs and bodies also seemed to come apart, like when you swim in the warm sea, in the calm, soft sea in the afternoon" (95).

Style is also used to create a sense of timelessness or eternity about the characters and their dilemmas. Thus, for example, Tere and her mother, "like always, the same as always" (167), remain in their apartment. As Antonio contemplates his home, the narrator tells us that "There is the house where he always returns, where he always gets into trouble, like in those terrible children's stories" (187); and when Antonio returns to his room at a *pensión*, he is uncertain whether to "submerge himself forever in that room" (235). In sum, the style and technique of *The Man of the Saints* form an important part of Fernández Santos's movement away from Social Realism. The stylistic and technical constructs of the novel transcend the limits imposed by the objective, third-person narrator of his earlier novels, coinciding generally with the novelistic tendencies in Spain during the late 1960s that seek new narrative forms and innovative means of expression.

Libro de las memorias de las cosas

Fernández Santos's fifth novel, *Libro de las memorias de las cosas* [The Book of Memorable Events], won the Premio Nadal in 1970. Although the literary prestige of the Nadal Prize had been increasingly diluted during the previous decade by the publisher's commercial interests, it nonetheless stimulated immediate critical interest in Fernández Santos's novel. Reviewers in general responded favorably to the work, further enhancing the author's return to prominence that began in 1969 with *The Man of the Saints*. As did the earlier work, *The Book of Memorable Events* evinces Fernández Santos's evolution away from his novels of Social Realism. This is not to say that he explicitly renounces the themes and technical constructs of his earlier fiction (e.g., realistic dialogue, the objective observation of external reality, a collective protagonist), but rather that he eliminates some elements and incorporates others as secondary components of a more complex narrative structure. At the same time, however, *The Book of Memorable Events* does not coincide with the mainstream of experimental fiction written in Spain during the 1960s (it does not, for example, advance an autotelic text or exhibit a tendency toward self-consciousness).[10] Instead, it reaffirms the movement of Fernández Santos's fiction toward the psychological probing of individual characters and their existential dilemmas.

As in the case of much of Fernández Santos's previous fiction, the origin of *The Book of Memorable Events* can be traced to the author's documentaries. After filming a small mountain village in northern Castille in the middle 1960s, Fernández Santos happened upon two partially obscured graves on the outskirts of the town. As he explained in his Salamanca lecture in 1971, "I asked who was buried there, and I was told a family of Protestants. In that deserted place, desolate and remote, those gravestones in that untilled field gave me a lot to think about."[11] The result of this "meditation," *The Book of Memorable Events*, portrays the growth and decline of a fictional Protestant community in Spain from the late 1800s to the present.[12] The novel is set in contemporary Spain and centers on Margarita and Virginia Sedano, daughters of the sect's founder, Luciano Sedano. Through the memories of Margarita, church documents, letters, and discussions among characters about the sect, the history of the community gradually emerges in fragmented fashion.

The title of the novel is derived from the Old Testament Book of Esther. Although the events of the narrative do not parallel those related in the Bible, the novel can be linked to Esther in two significant ways. First, it recounts the memorable events and deeds of the Brethren in Spain, corresponding to the historial chronicles read in Esther by King Xerxes. Second, it details the religious persecution suffered by Spanish Protestants and their struggle to survive, much in the same fashion that Esther relates the near extermination of the Jews. Although *The Book of Memorable Events* does not pretend to be historical in nature, it nonetheless provides an accurate portrayal of the abuse and suffering endured by Protestant communities in Spain during the past century.

The social concerns of *The Book of Memorable Events* lie implicit in the religious subject matter, but it should not be viewed as a theological or thesis novel. It probes a broad range of contemporary problems, from the religious conflict among the Brethren and the harassment of their community to the psychological and existential despair of Margarita and several other characters. Fernández Santos himself rejects the label "social novel," affirming that "Since I write novels, I wanted to write, and I ended up writing, a novel; not an essay, nor a doctrinal study, but purely and simply a novel."[13] He does not focus on biblical interpretation or the intricacies of religious doctrine, but on the critical problems encountered by Spanish Protestants in the face of an overwhelming Catholic majority. More importantly, however, he examines the personal dilemmas of the Brethren as they exist isolated from the mainstream of society, and he portrays the conflict between adherence to rigid Church doctrines and the desire for self-realization outside the sect. Margarita and Virginia Sedano clearly incarnate many of the problems confronted by the Brethren, but at the same time they embody the pervasive anguish and loneliness of contemporary life as a whole.

Although the novel is related from diverse points of view, it is through Margarita, who stands as the principal narrative consciousness, that the two dominant aspects of the text are shaped. First, through the evocation of her father, her father's first wife (Cecil), and certain aspects of her youth, she offers privileged information and personal insight into the history of the Brethren. Margarita's view of the world and her place within it have clearly been molded by her many years of service to the community. Now approaching middle age, she has adhered to the doctrines of the Brethren throughout her lifetime. Thus when her observations are combined with those of other narrators, a detailed historical accounting emerges. We learn, for example, of Luciano Sedano's efforts to expand and develop the community during its early years; of his marriage to Cecil and their role as spiritual leaders; of Luciano's struggle with the government and the Catholic Church for official recognition; of the cholera epidemic that nearly devastated the community. Luciano Sedano remains spiritually present for the Brethren long after his death, an inspirational figure for those attempting to preserve the sect and its beliefs.

The decline of the Brethren following the Civil War represents the most important "historical" focus of the novel. Fernández Santos does not explicitly delineate the causes of the decline, but they become evident as the work develops and a wide range of characters move in and out of the narrative. For example, since the sect exists primarily in small, rural villages, the population shift to larger cities has reduced the potential number of members. In addition, the changing religious climate in Spain inspires indifference among the youth, who are now unwilling to embrace the rigid behavioral and moral codes of the community (e.g., no smoking, no dancing, etc.). The sect is beset by internal conflict among its members, and its passive evangelism is threatened externally by more aggressive Protestant groups, such as the Jehovah's Witnesses. Fernández Santos introduces these problems not as extraneous elements aimed at enhancing a specific thesis, but rather as integral components of the historical framework of the novel. They are revealed both in the psychological conflicts of the characters and the diachronic view of twentieth-century Spanish society offered by the narrators.

In addition to her role as observer/historian, Margarita embodies a psychological and existential despair that dominates much of the novel. To a large degree, Margarita symbolizes the conflicts and doubts faced by the Brethren as a whole. She has lived isolated from society outside the community, she has been nurtured on the religious teachings of her parents, and she possesses no concrete understanding of the antagonistic forces that are undermining the existence of the community. Through-out her life she has been compelled to repress her social being as well as her desire to experience love and marriage. The root of her problem, however, lies less with religious doubt than with the profound discord that characterizes her familial relationships. On the one hand, she has elevated her father and Cecil to a plane of spiritual perfection, and her idealized memories of them enable her to mitigate the anguish and tension of the present. In contrast, her sister and mother inspire feelings of resentment and even hatred. The conflict between these figures in her life, coupled with her isolation within the community, creates severe psychological agitation for her, leading eventually to her mental collapse and suicide.

Margarita's repeated evocation of her father and Cecil is necessary for her to preserve her psychological well-being. Each is fixed in her memory as an idealized image that sustains her religious devotion. For example, she envisions her father more as a religious leader and symbol of goodness than as a parental figure of flesh and blood, as becomes evident in one of her interior monologues early in the novel. Although she has photographs of her father, she is unable to recall concrete features of his physical presence: "What was papa like? Rather tall or of medium height? Taller than Cecil, taller than mama. . . . And his eyes and the color of his hair? And his voice? It is difficult to remember. His voice and everything not suggested by the photograph disappear without leaving a trace."[14] This blurred memory of her father's physical being causes Margarita to envisage him as more than an ordinary parent. He becomes an abstract, symbolic figure who emerges in her memories as a biblical hero leading his flock to salvation. This is implied by the excerpt from Exodus that prefaces the novel,[15] and is explicitly articulated by Margarita as she recalls her father combating a plague of locusts (79–80). The biblical imagery and religious connotations of the incident clearly underscore Sedano's sanctified role among the Brethren, an image sustained after his death which directly affects the evolution of the community and Margarita's central role within it.

Fantasy and Change

Margarita evokes Cecil in her interior monologues more frequently than any other character. Although Cecil died several years before Margarita was born, Margarita feels more intimately tied to her than to her own mother or sister. First of all, the members of the community had always claimed that Virginia resembled Luciano Sedano, while Margarita bore a likeness to Cecil. Furthermore, Margarita maintains a latent resentment toward her own mother, who always seemed to favor Virginia. This hostility, implied throughout the novel, is revealed explicitly in one of Margarita's dreams, in which she strangles her mother while her father is away from home. Apart from these antagonistic feelings toward her natural mother, however, Margarita is attracted to Cecil for other reasons. Like Luciano, she stands as an idealized model of unwavering altruism. Cecil arrived in the community during the cholera epidemic bearing medicine and supplies from England. When she and Luciano later married, they served as inspirational figures for the community and promoted the missions of the Brethren throughout Spain.

More important than her religious activities, however, Cecil emerges as the principal figure to whom Margarita directs her reveries and fantasies. Margarita confesses to Cecil sentiments that she is unable to voice to anyone else: her religious indecision, her desire to discover the world outside of the community, her acute resentment of Virginia. Margarita beseeches Cecil to divulge the source of her spiritual strength, for Margarita's own religious commitment has become devitalized: "Tell me, Cecil, what is that courage like that you had, that they say you had; that voice that tells you in the night, in the worst hour, 'Your life is important and useful.' Tell me what it is like to spend hour after hour, night after night, holding your Bible" (96).

Margarita also confesses to Cecil her sexual frustrations, her sins of thought (if not of action), and her fears of growing old alone. Above all, she envisions Cecil as her only friend and source of guidance. "You are my only friend, comfort and hope, despite those cold and distant eyes. You know the truth even though you say nothing, you know well how I can be saved, no matter how hard, cruel, or difficult it may be" (379). Despite this intimacy, however, Cecil is unable to assuage Margarita's psychological agitation. On the contrary, the dead woman's recurrent presence not only reveals Margarita's emotional instability, but lays bare Margarita's life in all its existential anguish.

The suppression of Margarita's desire to discover the world is most intensely dramatized in her relationship with Virginia. While Margarita fantasizes about love and fears growing old without marrying, Virginia is concerned only with obeying and propagating the rigid moral codes of the community. Margarita's long-felt resentment of her sister intensifies as they grow old and reaches its climax during their trip to an ecumenical meeting of Spanish Protestants in Barcelona. During the drive to Barcelona with two other members of the Brethren, several important issues

are discussed. The conversation is dominated by the unorthodox views of
Agustín, who questions the practices of the community and points to the
decline in membership as proof that the Church should change its ways.
Margarita is first repulsed by Agustín's observations, then silently
admits that he may be correct. As the trip progresses she grows more
attracted to his dynamic personality and to his refusal to embrace
stultifying traditions. When they arrive in Barcelona, Margarita spends
the day with Agustín rather than attend the meetings. As the two drive
along the coast, she silently evokes Cecil and questions her about love.
Margarita fantasizes about the nature of love, but focuses most explicitly
on its absence in her life: "Love isn't the solitude of the apartment, with
its trains that cry; nor is it that other kind of loneliness of the library. The
solitude of visiting the sick, or the services in the chapel, or looking in
the mirror watching the years go by, the mirror in which, according to
mama, when you look at yourself the devil appears on the other side. I
don't know what [love] must be like, but I imagine that, from a certain
age on, it is not being so hard and so bitter like Virginia" (191).

During her drive with Agustín, Margarita feels liberated for the first
time in her life. When she returns the next morning to her room at the
hotel, however, Virginia slaps her. Virginia's angry reaction closely
parallels a scene that occurred when the two sisters were young and
Margarita had spoken with a boy (also named Agustín) from outside the
community. Although Margarita had passively accepted Virginia's action several years earlier, its repetition now impels her to defy Virginia's
influence and to reject the community as a whole. Indeed, rather than
attempt to balance the ways of the world with the doctrines of the
Brethren, Margarita concludes, "How small and limited [my] life is,
and how absurd it is to worry about what Virginia or the Brethren think"
(239—40).

Margarita's withdrawal from the community represents a process of
psychic individuation that is at once painful and liberating. She seeks to
experience society at the same time that she severs her connections with
the past. Her life centers on the hope of seeing Agustín again, but she is
consumed by her solitary existence apart from the Brethren. She moves
into a room by herself and refuses to communicate with Virginia; she
buys new clothes and no longer attends church. Still, however, she fails
to gain love or happiness. We learn, in fact, that her entire life has
developed as an unfulfilled fantasy. From her childhood dreams of
working as a missionary in far-off countries, to her most recent love for
Agustín, Margarita has invented and pursued a notion of happiness that
has consistently eluded her. When she finally realizes that Agustín will

not return to see her, she grows physically and emotionally ill. Eventually, she is warned that she will be expelled from the community if she does not attend Church. Her recurrent insomnia now becomes debilitating, and her tension and resentment intensify until she finally confesses to Cecil, "There came a day, a night, when I couldn't abhor myself more" (380).

Margarita's suicide represents the most radical response of any of Fernández Santos's characters to the emptiness and anguish of their existence. Margarita does not take her life merely out of frustration for her present situation, but out of despair for her future as well. Despite her rejection of the community and her previous way of life, the present remains so choked off by the stagnant past that there is no place in it for the future. Margarita's suicide is not motivated by guilt for what she has done, but by her realization of what she is unable to do—actualize her existence either within or outside of the religious and social confines of the community. Her repudiation of the Brethren and their codes of behavior places the entire responsibility for her existence squarely on her own shoulders. Realizing that her future will echo the emptiness of her past, she opts for self-destruction. She thus becomes the most tragic of Fernández Santos's characters, but, at the same time, the one who most forcefully determines her own destiny.

Secular vs. Religious Life

In contrast to Margarita, Virginia adheres strictly to Church doctrine and works to maintain the traditions of the community. Her life has been molded both by the importance of her father to the history of the community and by the intensity of her own faith. Throughout the novel she functions as the antithesis of Margarita, never displaying the religious or existential doubt that plagues her sister. During most of the narrative Virginia appears to the reader through the consciousness of Margarita, who views her sister as an obstacle to self-fulfillment. Only during the final third of the novel are we permitted to enter directly into the consciousness of Virginia, and though she grows more psychologically complex as her thoughts are divulged, she emerges for the most part as the same religiously devout figure portrayed by Margarita.

As does her sister, Virginia fears above all a solitary existence. This fear of loneliness and the desire for companionship reveal the secular and emotional elements of Virginia's being, which in turn give breadth and depth to her character. In her relationship with Margarita, she eventually admits to the sin of pride and even negligence, and ponders her own guilt in provoking Margarita to abandon the community. At the same time, however, she continues to uphold the canons of the community, affirming that her sister must be punished if she disobeys the Church. Thus when Margarita commits suicide Virginia is psychologically devastated, for she feels responsible for Margarita's death. Virginia also abandons the community and spends several months in a sanatorium before returning to her small hometown to begin life anew. Clearly, Fernández Santos does not cast Virginia as a symbol of religious fanaticism, nor does he manipulate her to sustain a social or moral thesis. Instead, he develops her character so that her actions and thoughts are psychologically credible, conveying realistically the dilemmas and consequences of her life within the community.

The most explicit dichotomy in the novel between good and evil, spiritual sublimation and carnal desire, centers on Molina and a woman known simply as the "demonio." Once a devout member of the community, Molina is expelled both for his failure to attend religious services and for his illicit relationship with the young woman. Molina and his demon eventually move away from the community and seek help in a mining venture from Molina's wealthy brother. After spending several months in a small mountain village in Asturias, the two lovers begin to despise one another. Molina eventually returns to reading his Bible, while his demon carries on an affair with the son of Molina's brother. When the mine fails to produce the anticipated wealth, the demon steals Molina's money and flees to Madrid.

At first glance the story of Molina and his demon conveys a moral that would seem to coincide with a thesis novel. The woman incarnates evil and reifies sins of the flesh, while Molina represents the parishioner led astray by temptation. However, at the same time that this parable unfolds, Fernández Santos develops the two characters in such a way that they possess individual identities, desires, and doubts. Thus the demon is not merely an evil woman, but also a deprived child raised in poverty and abused by a series of men for whom she worked. The hardships of her youth are revealed in order to demonstrate the importance of the past in her actions of the present. Her entire life, it is suggested, has been molded by her obsession to escape poverty. She is attracted to Molina because she found him different from other men, and "she thought that he could finally change her life, her destiny" (53). In terms of character development, then, Fernández Santos initially establishes Molina's demon as merely a symbol of evil by not giving her a name. As the narrative progresses, however, she emerges as a complex round character, with individual traits and specific motivations for her actions.

Molina similarly evolves as a highly individualized character, though the motivations for his rejection of the community and his attraction to the demon are never made clear: "It was he who had sought her out . . . perhaps in an effort to free himself forever from the Brethren, or perhaps from the memory of his wife, or perhaps to escape from himself, as in death, as in premature destruction" (204). As the novel develops he becomes dominated by the woman and works in the mine only to satisfy her demands, admitting that he both desires her and needs her, but also recognizing that she has come to dominate every aspect of his life. He thus despises her at the same time that he submits to her control. After she steals his money and flees, Molina eventually returns to the community and marries Virginia. Fernández Santos, however, does not depict their marriage as the triumph of good over evil, but rather as the union of two anguished individuals who have turned to one another out of existential solitude and necessity.

Other characters enhance the historical aspects of the novel more than the psychological. In many instances they incarnate specific problems that have heightened the deterioration of the community since the Civil War. For example, the intellectual energies of Múñoz are directed toward establishing a school for the children of the community. His efforts are met with indifference by the other Brethen, however, and the project never develops. While Múñoz ponders the faith of other youths of the community, his own two children explore alternative religious principles. His daughter Adela attends the University of Madrid and grows attracted to a young Jehovah's Witness. She admires the Witnesses both for their active evangelism and the refusal to compromise their beliefs (e.g., they choose imprisonment over military service). While the Brethren continue to diminish in size, the Witnesses increase their numbers each year through the vigorous recruitment of new members. Thus Adela's repudiation of the community represents less a rejection of its beliefs than a desire to participate in a more vital religious experience. She opts for the aggressive zeal of the Witnesses, denouncing her own community and its passive acceptance of eventual dissolution.

Múñoz's son, Arturo, represents another aspect of the problem faced by the Brethren. Similar to many young persons, his introduction to life outside the community inspires doubt about his religious convictions. He admits that he would like to profess absolute faith, but explains to his father that "the time has passed when you could say or proclaim, 'This is like this, this isn't, this is the truth, this is sin.' I assure you that before condemning anyone, either among ourselves or from the outside, those who we call 'from the world,' I would give it a lot of thought, I would be very careful" (300). Agustín, another peripheral character and likewise disenchanted with the present lassitude of the Brethren, advocates a more active evangelism. His ideas influence Margarita profoundly, but have little impact on the rest of the community. Emilio represents still another aspect of the community. Although once an engaged intellectual, he now reflects the pervasive abulia of the Brethren and their sterility of thought and action. In sum, Fernández Santos moves his minor characters in and out of the narrative as representatives of specific historical and religious problems encountered by the Brethren. Although they do not emerge as round, fully developed characters, they nonetheless complement the principal figures of the novel by enhancing the complexity and diversity of the atmosphere in which they move.

Style and Technique

The technical and stylistic elements of *The Book of Memorable Events* reflect the author's continued movement away from the objective narrative of Social Realism. Recalling his style of *The Man of the Saints*, Fernández Santos develops a more fluid prose that stands in marked contrast to the elliptic narrative of his first three novels. Also as in *The Man of the Saints*, he demonstrates a preference for grouping adjectives, nouns, and verbs into groups of three when portraying external social phenomena or psychological traits of the characters. This not only creates a more complex reality characterized by fine distinctions of meaning, but frequently results in the amplification or intensification of the particular subject at hand. Since dialogue scarcely appears in the novel, Fernández Santos is able to establish a rhythmic flow that closely aligns his prose with the peripatetic style of much of the new Spanish narrative of the 1970s.

Fernández Santos introduces several technical innovations that distinguish *The Book of Memorable Events* from his earlier fiction. Although he divides the narrative into short segments similar to those found in *The Untamed*, most of the technical constructs are intended to produce a more complex novelistic reality than found in the earlier work. This is especially evident in the multiple narrative perspectives that often undermine the reliability of a particular narrator. For example, Margarita explains to a newspaper reporter that she and her sister left their small village several years before in order to provide better medical care for their father. As Margarita recounts certain events from the past, however, Fernández Santos interpolates an anonymous "voice of the town" (e.g., pp. 361−62; 369−70) that contradicts Margarita's story.

Although the reader cannot determine whose account is more accurate, the very existence of the "voice" impairs Margarita's role as a reliable narrator, undermining the objective reality that would otherwise be conveyed through her interview with the reporter.

In addition to the "voice of the town," several other points of view are offered: Church documents, letters, flashbacks, dialogues, first-person narrations of several characters. The inclusion of the reporter writing the story on the community also provides a new perspective, since Margarita relates to him a brief oral history of the Brethren. This combination of narrative techniques enhances the sociohistorical complexities of the novel (i.e., we view the rise and decline of the Brethren in a temporally fragmented order), and provides a diversity of insights into the psychological makeup of the characters. As a consequence, the novel stands diametrically opposed to the narrative of objective realism of the 1950s. Coupled with *The Man of the Saints*, it represents the author's most acute probing of individual characters who are consistently estranged from meaning and fulfillment.

Fernández Santos also creates in *The Book of Memorable Events* a certain amount of intrigue which, with the exception of *The Untamed*, is generally absent from his previous works. As the novel progresses Margarita's neurotic personality emerges in a series of interior monologues. Her religious and existential conflicts intensify her insomnia and she frequently becomes physically ill. The discord with her sister grows more acute and Margarita is warned that she may be expelled from the community. As the narrative reaches its climax, Fernández Santos intensifies Margarita's psychological and physical stress to such a degree that she seems to lose complete control of her emotions and actions. At this point a narrative segment abruptly ends, and another begins with the reporter visiting a sanatorium in search of one of the Sedano sisters. The narrative is structured here so that the reader associates the sanatorium with Margarita's emotional collapse. The segment begins with the doctor at the institution explaining to the reporter the severity of the woman's condition upon her arrival there. "She refused to do anything: eat, go for a walk or even work like the other women. She would just sit there, upstairs in her room, and look out her window. She was practically a vegetable" (381). Fernández Santos clearly intends for the reader to believe that Margarita has been placed in the sanatorium. It is finally revealed, however, that the patient is Virginia, and that Margarita has died under mysterious circumstances. Although somewhat incongruous with the slow pace and introspective monologues that characterize much of the narrative, this unexpected revelation reminds us that the author is present to manipulate events and structure the plot to attain maximum dramatic and artistic effect.

Although *The Book of Memorable Events* expresses certain thematic concerns that appear in Fernández Santos's novels of Social Realism (e.g., the sterility of life in small villages, the decline of religion, the harsh physical environment of rural Spain), it nonetheless illustrates the author's continuing evolution away from the constructs of his earlier narrative. The fluid and complex style, the multiple narrative perspectives, and the psychological probing of his characters parallel many of the innovative tendencies initiated in *The Man of the Saints* and reaffirm the new focus of the author's fiction. At the same time, however, Fernández Santos demonstrates in *The Book of Memorable Events* an interest in pursuing diversified narrative possibilities. He creates what can be termed a "fictional history," in which he constructs a fictive world rooted in historical fact (i.e., the Protestants in Spain). This interest in fictional history is maintained throughout the 1970s in three books of short stories (*Las catedrales*, *Paraíso encerrado*, and *A orillas de una vieja dama*), and it forms the cornerstone of his next three novels, *La que no tiene nombre* (1977), *Extramuros* (1979), and *Cabrera* (1981). In each of these works Fernández Santos explores the distant past and develops his narrative toward a commingling of historical realism and what he terms "a literature of imagination."[16]

Chapter Four

Toward a Literature
of Imagination

La que no tiene nombre

Fernández Santos published his sixth novel, *La que no tiene nombre* [The One Who Has No Name], in the spring of 1977. Although it does not form part of the experimental Spanish narrative of the 1970s, it does coincide with the general movement away from the forms and themes of Social Realism that prevailed during the previous two decades. More importantly, however, within Fernández Santos's own corpus of works *The One Who Has No Name* affirms a continued resolve by the author to avoid literary stasis. The Neo-realistic canons that mold his first three novels, and the existential and psychological analysis of individuals characterizing *The Man of the Saints* and *The Book of Memorable Events*, now yield to a kind of narrative that the author himself terms "a literature of imagination." Fernández Santos does not attempt in *The One Who Has No Name* to crystallize reality through photographic mimesis or psychological revelation, but rather probes beneath the surface of reality to lay bare the more profound and enigmatic elements that lie beneath.

It is important to bear in mind, however, that Fernández Santos's modified literary approach in *The One Who Has No Name* does not imply a rejection of his previous mode of writing. Indeed, several important elements that appear in much of his earlier fiction recur as integral components of the narrative. For example, the creation of a fictive history of an area, which forms the nucleus of *The One Who Has No Name*, has its roots in *The Untamed* (1954) and is developed most explicitly in *The Book of Memorable Events* (1971). In addition, the physical milieu of *The One Who Has No Name*, set in a mountain valley of northern León, is similar to the area portrayed in several of the author's previous works. Also important in both *The One Who Has No Name* and earlier novels is the central role of geographical determinism. Life for the people of the mountains has continually been molded by the harsh physical environment, while recurrent isolation has conditioned the psyche of the inhabitants and shaped their view of existence. In short, many fundamental thematic tenets of Fernández Santos's prior fiction are sustained in *The One Who Has No Name*, although they appear in different narrative forms and are developed from diverse points of view. This can be seen both in their juxtaposition to new ideas and through a unique diachronic perspective in the novel that spans five centuries.

Fernández Santos constructs three distinct stories in *The One Who Has No Name*, narratives that take place during three different time periods. Each story shares the same physical setting, but develops its own set of characters who possess individual problems and conflicts. The most important tale relates the life of a legendary medieval woman named Juana García, known simply as the Dama. Imprisoned by her father for refusing his incestuous desires, she eventually yields to his advances to escape the tower in which she is confined. Later, when King Ferdinand and Queen Isabel assemble an army to challenge the territorial claims of Alfonso of Portugal, she volunteers to serve and goes off to battle disguised as a man. After demonstrating her valor at the battle of Toro in 1476, she is knighted by the king. As she rides home to León, however, she is murdered along the road by a group of jealous soldiers. The Dama's story is narrated in the first person by her longtime servant, who witnessed her incestuous relationship with her father and accompanied her to Toro. As the narrative progresses the servant interpolates into his story fragments of a medieval ballad that recount the Dama's life and convey the themes of incest and the "lady warrior."[1]

Against the backdrop of the Leonese mountains and the legendary Dama two tales unfold in a more contemporary setting. The first takes place shortly after the Civil War (1936—39) and relates the experiences of an exiled teacher who returns to the mountains of León as an anti-Franco guerrilla. The teacher attempts to organize a small band of men in order eventually to inspire a popular uprising. Despite his efforts, he encounters only frustration and failure. When his men are massacred during a bank robbery, the teacher realizes that he is incapable of weakening the government's power, and thus decides to return to France.

The other story, set in the immediate present, is divided into two closely related subplots. The first revolves around an old man (known as the "grandfather" throughout the novel) and his son-in-law (called the "father" throughout) who live in the mountains of the legendary Dama. Each year they are isolated from the outside world and from one another during the harsh months of winter. The two have been antagonists since the grandson (son of the father) abandoned the mountains several years before, and they refuse to communicate during their long months of solitude. During the current winter the old man spends his time shoveling a path through the snow in the general direction of a distant snowplow. The father hunts every day, watching from a distance the movements of the grandfather. As the novel progresses both men die. The son-in-law accidentally shoots himself, and the old man is bitten by a wild animal while burying his son-in-law's body. At the same time that this drama is acted out on the mountain, the second subplot advances in the provincial capital. The grandson who had left the mountains sells real estate and waits for the two men to die so that he can deal their land to foreign developers. As the narrative clearly reveals, however, the grandson's life parallels the unproductive and solitary existence of his father and grandfather. He idles away the time in a local nightclub and carries on a disagreeable affair with his mistress.

The Legendary Dama

Although the latter two stories form an integral part of the novel, its thematic intensity and principal anecdotal interest stem from the Dama. Fernández Santos's invention of the legendary woman has its source in the author's real-life experience. In his travels through northern León he frequently came across a coat of arms belonging to a figure lost in medieval history. Using the coat of arms as a point of departure, he created the legend of the Dama, and was later requested by his editor at Ediciones Destino to expand it into a novel.[2] He opted to include the story as only one part of a larger project, however, and thus *The One Who Has No Name* came into being in its present form. As were many of his other novels, therefore, *The One Who Has No Name* is rooted in the author's travels and is set in an area of Spain with which he is intimately acquainted.

The impetus within the novel for the narration of the Dama's life stems from the annual performance of a play depicting her legendary deeds. We are not permitted to view the play, performed by the schoolchildren of the area, but learn of the Dama's life through the narration of her servant. The narrative present for these segments is thus the fifteenth century, and both the language of the servant and the interpolated ballad underscore the pervasive medieval ambience. For the most part, the servant relates elements from the Dama's life that enhance her legendary fame: the forced incestuous relationship with her father; the resentment felt by her mother and sisters; the march to join the king's fight against the Portuguese; her skill and valor as a soldier; her murder while returning home. The legend of the Dama is told in such a way, however, that it transcends the specific components of its content. That is, the Dama gradually comes to embody the principal thematic concern of the novel ("the one who has no name;" i.e., death), and the ambiguous nature of her real-life existence intensifies the enigmatic milieu of the mountains.

The Dama first encounters death while on her way to join the king's army. As she crosses a bridge she comes upon two thieves dangling at the end of a rope, while "the one who has no name" waits nearby. The Dama converses with Death, who reminds her that "Nobody seeks me out on his own volition."[3] The personification of death here clearly brings the legend of the Dama to the edge of allegory. As time passes, the lady encounters "the one who has no name" several more times and gradually becomes identified with it. For example, in a minor skirmish with a band of ruffians the Dama forms around her a "circle of death" (137), and her furious fighting transforms her into a "wind of death that split open heads without pity" (137). Later, Death follows the army as it marches toward Toro and watches from the river bank when the battle finally takes place. As the fighting grows in intensity and scores of soldiers are slain, the Dama finds herself not only surrounded by death, but suddenly she is fused with it in a complete allegorical correspondence. As the servant recalls, "[The one who had no name] turned to look at me. Yet it wasn't the nameless, but rather the Dama . . ." (218).

Not until the end of the novel, however, does the unique commingling of the Dama and Death come into clear focus. We learn that in the present-day legend the lady is referred to as the "Dama" by some persons and as "the one who has no name" by others, because her name has been effaced from the coat of arms. That is, the contemporary inhabitants of the mountains do not know the name Juana García. By the time the reader discovers this logical explanation for the Dama's two names, however, the allegorical connotation of "the one who has no name" is already firmly established. Hence the Dama as "the one who has no name" and the "Dama-as-death" remain confounded in the narrative. Moreover, the Dama/death synthesis appears in the other two stories, and therefore becomes the central motif of the novel through its diachronic enhancement of theme.

Integration of the Narratives

Although much of the anecdotal interest of the novel centers on the Dama, the other two stories do not rely upon the legendary figure for the development of plot, character, or social criticism. The narrative of each story is interspersed among the other two, but each of the narrative fragments is treated as a fictional present, without reference to the episodes that immediately precede and follow it. For example, when the exiled teacher returns to the Leonese mountains shortly after the Civil War, the political implications of his intentions—opposition to Franco—need not be viewed in relation to the other two stories in order to be understood. Likewise, the social content of the grandfather-father-son episodes (e.g., the isolation of rural Spanish villages, poverty, the selling of land to foreign investors) reflects contemporary societal problems and does not depend upon the other two stories for its critical impact. At the same time, however, each story is linked to the others in several important ways, all serving to enhance theme and illustrate the deep meaning of the narrative.

In the first place, Fernández Santos creates in *The One Who Has No Name* a milieu shared by the inhabitants of the mountainous area over the course of centuries. The valley of Las Hoces is isolated from life outside the mountains, and both the psychological and physical ambience comprise a pervasive desolation, ruin, and fatalism. As with Juan Rulfo's Comala or Juan Benet's Región, there exists in the valley a direct relationship between the geographical location, harsh climatic conditions, and physical ruin on the one hand, and the omnipresent specter of death and ultimate abrogation of human existence on the other. Fernández Santos not only links the three stories by recurrent use of specific descriptions of the mountains, but affirms the influence of geographical determinism from the Middle Ages to the present.

Several cyclical patterns are established among the three stories through the repetition of meteorological and geographical images. For example, the mountain valley of Las Hoces can be entered through a single pass, which is frequently blocked by snow. Hence the area is cut off from the lowlands for several months each year. This is true not only for the medieval residents of the area, but for the contemporary inhabitants as well. In addition to enduring continual isolation and estrangement, the villagers are devitalized by the physical ruin of the area. Similar to the barren land depicted in *The Untamed* and *In the Fire*, the valley of Las Hoces consists of "sterile soil" (54, 99, 111, etc.) that condemns the inhabitants to a continual cycle of poverty. The physical condition of the small village stands as a distressing symbol of pervasive decadence: "The entire gray wall of ruins makes visible the damaged roofs, the broken walls, the empty hinges, the rafters burned by the ice. Everywhere, only the frozen movement of the jackdaws, and the constant dripping on every caved-in roof, on every eaves about to collapse" (75).

The frigid power of the *cierzo* ("cold northerly wind") also shapes life in the area. It has effaced the name of the village from an old metal sign (the symbolism here is obvious), and makes life uncomfortable for all of the residents, regardless of their social status or the historical period in which they live. The image of the wind, threaded throughout each of the three stories, is gradually anthropomorphized and comes to symbolize the area's hostile reaction to its human inhabitants. It makes the mountains inhospitable for the early medieval settlers; it plagues the guerrillas as they hide in the mountains after the Civil War; it threatens the very existence of the two old men attempting to survive the winter. Other natural elements form a similar bonding of past and present. The threatening clouds that hover above the valley in the present are the same clouds that covered the area during the Middle Ages and will continue to cover it for centuries to come: ". . . and the clouds above, in an endless procession, as if going around the world, return and make their appearance once more" (61). The winter storms that isolate the valley from the outside world also form a link between the centuries. The snow that blanketed the medieval inhabitants continues to envelop the area today. As the third-person narrator tells us (in the present) concerning the past: "The snow kept falling, year after year, more and more like a blanket, just like now. And like now, it covered the stables and the people" (30).

Since the mountain valley of Las Hoces is portrayed over a period of five centuries, temporal flow forms a crucial aspect of the novel. Manipulation of time as theme links the three stories in much the same way as do the geographical and climatic elements. Most importantly, Fernández Santos dismisses the notion of the pastness of the past, both in his thematic vision and in the development of character. In the former, the passing of time leads to the inevitable finality of death, conveyed in the novel through the bonding of Dama-death-time within the geographical confines of the mountains across each of the time periods. On the one hand, the valley is suspended in a rarefied atmosphere where the influence of external time (e.g., technology, progress, etc.) has been annulled. But the insulation from external time does not impede the forward temporal flow that impels the individual toward inevitable extinction. Fernández Santos focuses on death to some extent in his previous novels (e.g., Miguel's tuberculosis in *In the Fire*, Margarita's suicide in *The Book of Memorable Events*), but only as a secondary element of a broader existential vision. In *The One Who Has No Name*, death and time converge into a cosmic force that defines the essence of existence in the mountains. This is explicitly affirmed in the final segment of the novel by the mythical coalescence of Dama/Death and time: "As the blizzard grows in intensity . . . the Dama and time grow near and fuse with one another until they disappear up the path, continuing onward to the highest peaks of the mountains" (242). Hence the deaths that occur in each of the three stories (those of the Dama, the guerrillas, the two old men) represent the inevitable tragedy associated with life in the mountains and, at the same time, extend this tragedy across time periods.

Fernández Santos's portrayal of time in the novel, and the correlative notion of fatalistic destiny, also affects the psyche of the characters on an individual level. The Dama reflects on her prolonged imprisonment and concludes that she will spend the rest of her life in the tower unless she yields to her father's incestuous desires. Her father, meanwhile, seeks to deceive time (death) and regain his youth by sleeping with his daughter. The guerrilla leader is haunted by memories of the past (especially his failure at the seminary), and links the useless wars of history with his own futile activities in the present. But the two characters most oppressed by time are the father and grandfather, whose perception of temporal flow is limited primarily to the cyclical pattern of autumn freeze and spring thaw. Their self-contained world in the mountains seals them from the external influence of time, but also condemns them to the eternal cycle of death that has defined existence in the mountains for more than five centuries.

The grandfather is conscious of his isolation from external time, and thus spends his days digging toward a snow plow stalled farther down the mountain. He shovels through the snow not simply in order to communicate with the outside world, but "to fill the day, prolong it . . ." (28). In order to give a semblance of order and temporal perspective to his life, the grandfather relies upon the flow of smoke from the father's distant chimney. Without the smoke he is at times unable to distinguish between night and day. Fernández Santos further heightens the grandfather's uncalibrated sense of time by employing certain stylistic variations in the narrative. For example, when describing the old man's activities he frequently uses infinitives in nominal phrases, conveying a sense of perpetual stasis: "Dig, cut, push the shovel with his foot, a bit more, fill the day, prolong it, keep on splitting it into parts, like the mud at his feet . . ." (28).[4] In contrast, the physical environment that surrounds him is made dynamic by the use of conjugated verbs: "The wind carries the sound of bells . . . now and then a whirlwind of snow leaps by . . . the north wind comes down threateningly" (28–29).

   This disparity between the active movement of natural elements and
the stagnant life of the grandfather is further underscored by the author's
use of the passive voice when summarizing the grandfather's daily
activities: "The open road is looked at . . . the calculation is made . . .
memory is frozen and one returns over one's own footsteps already
hardened again" (28). The use of the passive construction here and in
other instances points to a schism between the grandfather and his
actions. That is, it not only suggests the continuous repetition of the old
man's activities but also implies that he is unable to control the course of
his life. Indeed, his existence is engulfed by an ongoing mythical flow of
time and events in the mountains that allows the individual only a
passive role in a tragic destiny.
   On occasion, the grandfather passes time in the present by allowing
his mind to drift into the past. He evokes the murder of his daughter's
lover by his jealous son-in-law, recalling the dead man's burial under the
manure of their stable. Yet for the most part, "Time and memory,
people and dates, even his own presence was confused" (176). Both he
and his son-in-law (i.e., the father) exist in a temporal trajectory
divorced from length and pace. Each acts out his life not because he is
impelled by reason or purpose, but because he forms part of a living
myth, with its origins in the Middle Ages, that is perpetuated through
him. The father and grandfather live chronologically in the present, yet
their existence barely differs from the life and times of the Dama. Only
the distant snow plow and a transistor radio suggest that the two men do
not live during the fifteenth century. Therefore, though they are tran-
sient figures in an eternal and unchanging universe of time, they are also
"immortal like the river, the hills, and the bridges" (94).
   Fernández Santos links the characters of the stories in several other
ways as well. The Dama frequently appears in the other two narratives,
implicitly through theme and explicitly within the thoughts of the
characters. She is evoked both as pseudohistorical legend and in her
allegorized form of death. For example, as the guerrilla leader moves
about the mountains to avoid contact with the civil guards, he wonders if
the area is the same now as during the time of the Dama. When his band
of men is killed outside the bank, he flees into the mountains in despair
over his failure. He again evokes the Dama and relates her life to his
own: "Sometimes he felt forsaken, like the Dama in the story that he
told countless times to his students; that Dama who . . . [fought] in a
useless war which did nothing to change the valley, who is remembered
only because she wasn't a man, and whose body is not to be found
anywhere if not in legend or in the common grave of history books"

(186). The grandfather is also tied to the Dama, although his awareness of her transcends legend. As he contemplates the snow and wind around him, he hears the distant voices of school children rehearsing the play of the Dama's life. The woman's heroic deeds fill his thoughts, yet she is soon transformed into her allegorical being. When he is bitten by the wild animal while burying his son-in-law, he feels "the nameless," (176) gnawing at his wound. When he later enters the son-in-law's house, Death sits on the steps awaiting their final encounter.

The son-in-law is similarly linked to the Dama's dual role as legendary figure and personified death. More specifically, he forms part of the hunter motif interwoven throughout the narrative and correlated with death. The importance of the hunt is rooted in the story of the Dama, whose father frequently rode about the countryside with his hunting falcon. What her father eventually kills, however, is not an animal, but a man (i.e., a hunter) who had set a trap for a fallow deer (*dama* in Spanish). Later, the Dama (as warrior) becomes a hunter of men, and her servant relates that she began "killing for the sake of killing" (137). The son-in-law (father), a present-day hunter, likewise "seeks to kill for the sake of killing" (21), noting that he could do away with the grandfather as easily as he could shoot a deer. It is ironic, of course, that the son-in-law's death is caused by his own gun. More importantly, however, he is linked to death once again through the allegorized Dama. As he lies bleeding in the snow not far from his house, "a voice without a name, unknown, empty, returned" (119). Clearly, he no longer merely resembles the Dama as a hunter, but has come to coincide with her in death.

The different time periods and stories of the novel are also related in more general ways. For example, except for the Dama (Juana García) none of the characters is given a name. Hence the guerrilla leader, grandfather, father, and grandson, as well as several minor characters, emerge as archetypal figures representative of the particular mythology of the mountains. Each is consumed by a cosmic emptiness that is reified by the oppressive physical milieu. Another link among the stories centers on the wars that have repeatedly afflicted the area. From the Dama's participation in the war with Portugal, through the Carlist struggles of the nineteenth century and the Civil War of the Franco era, the mountains have been scarred by death. It is "the one who has no name," however, who most accurately defines these conflicts: "All [wars] are just and unjust at the same time. All are foolish and holy. There is always a criminal and an executioner. You're lucky if you pick the right side. Pick the right side or know how to wait, the same as in life" (101).

The One Who Has No Name is divided into short narrative segments (of generally three or four pages) that alternate among the three principal stories and time periods. These divisions help to establish a tempo in the novel that enhances both intrigue and theme. The former emerges as a result of the pseudoserialization of plot. That is, at a crucial (or at least suspenseful) moment of the story (e.g., the Dama is wounded in battle; the son-in-law is shot by his own gun; the guerrilla leader flees after his men are killed), the narrative may be broken while the next segment of one of the other stories continues. Similar to the anticipation technique employed in *The Untamed*, this fragmentation of plot is designed to sustain suspense in the manner of traditional novelistic design. At the same time, however, the juxtaposition of certain segments of one story with those of another intensifies theme or creates irony through the association of ideas and actions in contiguous scenes. For example, the account of the Dama's bravery in a skirmish with the enemy is followed by a description of the guerrillas' attack on three old men driving through the mountains in a battered Ford. The disparity between the two incidents (i.e., the valor and skill of the Dama versus the petty thievery of the guerrillas) is not only humorous, but also underscores the sterility of the guerrillas' actions and their failure to disrupt the government. Other contiguous scenes are equally poignant: the Dama's father kills a laborer for setting a trap on his lands (22−25), while in the next scene the son-in-law (hunter) murders his wife's lover (25−27). Death observes the Dama and other soldiers march along a river bank (191−194), and in the following fragment death appears in the son-in-law's house waiting for the grandfather. The Dama is confined in the tower by her father (51−54), while in the next segment the woman at the inn must acquiesce to the owner (i.e., she is essentially a prisoner at the inn) in order to survive. Hence Fernández Santos's structuring of the narrative fragments is aimed not only at creating intrigue within each story, but also furthers the thematic movement of the novel through the association of ideas across time periods.

Multiple narrative points of view serve to create a more complex novelistic reality. The first-person narration of the servant conveys a tone of detached historicity regarding the Dama's life that lends credibility and realism to what has been an invention of legend. The other two stories are related for the most part by an omniscient narrator, whose vision of the mysterious mountains and their enigmatic powers shapes the thematic emphasis of ruin, isolation, and death. But in contrast to his early novels of Social Realism, in which an objective point of view prevails, and to his probing of the individual in *The Man of the Saints* and *The Book of Memorable Events* through the frequent use of interior monologue, Fernández Santos now draws the reader into the portentous mood of *The One Who Has No Name* by utilizing narrative viewpoints outside the bounds of traditional realism. For example, following her death the Dama relates from her grave how she came to be killed. It is as if she aims to set the record straight now that, "My life no longer belongs to me; it is up there on the coat of arms that portrays me as a fully armed horseman" (224). Likewise, the murdered lover relates the manner in which he was killed and his subsequent experiences as a buried corpse (98—100). This kind of narrative diversity enhances milieu by transcending normal conventions of realism, and represents for Fernández Santos a break with his previous technical constructs. Although the use of dead narrators by no means offers an entirely innovative narrative approach within Hispanic fiction as a whole, Fernández Santos's willingness to expand and modify his techniques clearly indicates his continued evolution away from the more restrictive literary canons that impel the course of his fiction during the 1950s and 1960s.

Extramuros

Extramuros [Outside the Walls] achieved best-seller status in Spain during 1979 and went through several printings within the first few months of its publication.[5] It is the first of Fernández Santos's novels to attain such popular appeal, and has accorded him the broad public recognition sought since his early years as a novelist. The popularity of the work would seem to be the result of several factors. For one thing, it initiated a new series (entitled "The Four Seasons") of Editorial Argos Vergara, and therefore received extensive publicity and critical attention. Second, it focuses on controversial issues of seventeenth-century Spain that at once pique the prurient interest of the contemporary reader and satisfy intellectual and literary demands as well. As Joaquim Marco observed in his review of the novel: "The necessary elements are not lacking: hunger, mysticism, opposition between a rich and noble novitiate and a professed nun of the middle class, self-inflicted wounds, lesbianism, religious mysticism, Inquisition and trials."[6] A controversial topic such as lesbianism among nuns or trial by the Inquisition, related in a fluid, accessible style, no doubt have had much to do with the book's success. Yet by no means should *Outside the Walls* be linked to the mass of voyeuristic literature that has exploited the new freedom of expression in post-Franco Spain. On the contrary, it stands as a serious literary work that reaffirms the progression of Fernández Santos's fiction toward a literature of imagination.

The synthesis of history and imagination animating much of Fernández Santos's narrative during the 1970s forms the nucleus of *Outside the Walls*. But rather than offer a fragmented temporal structure that alternates between medieval legend and postwar Spain, as in *The One Who Has No Name*, Fernández Santos concentrates the action of *Outside the Walls* completely during the distant past. Both temporal and geographic incertitude prevail throughout the novel, but extratextual allusions suggest that the story is set in central Spain during the late sixteenth or early seventeenth century. While such ambiguity implies that Fernández Santos does not wish to re-create fictionally a specific historical occurrence, he offers sufficient insight into the social and political turmoil of the epoch and the role of the Inquisition to create historical verisimilitude. Thus the novel offers a detailed portrait of a society in crisis and, at the same time, reveals the profound psychological conflict of individual characters.

The plot of *Outside the Walls* develops linearly, with few digressions or unexpected twists. The story revolves around the lesbian relationship between two nuns (both unnamed, as are all the characters) living in a convent plagued by severe financial hardship. Narrated almost entirely in the first person by one of the nuns, the novel focuses on two interrelated problems: first, the amorous relationship between the two nuns and the psychological agitation of the narrator; second, the attempt by the narrator's lover to rescue the convent from ruin by conspiring to "create" a miracle. With the aid of the narrator, the nun has identical wounds cut into each of her hands and permits the other nuns to believe that the cuts have been made by God (i.e., they represent the wounded hands of Christ when he was nailed to the cross). The wounded hands soon become a major source of disruption within the convent as the nuns dispute their origin and meaning. Eventually, the drought and plague that have afflicted the area begin to attenuate, and for a short time conditions improve within the convent. This improvement is attributed to the miraculous wounds, which have become a symbol of God's favor. The nun's fame as a saint and healer spreads throughout the countryside, and masses of people visit the convent to catch a glimpse of her or to touch her hands.

The two plot centers of the novel (the lesbianism of the two nuns and the miraculous hands of the "saint") develop simultaneously and are intimately linked by the meditations of the nun/narrator. As the saint's hands become an increasingly divisive issue in the convent, the narrator experiences intense guilt for her own role in the deception. She continues to desire her lover, however, and the fear of their separation prevents her from revealing the truth. When the daughter of the convent's founder and benefactor (the Duke) chooses to pursue a religious life at the now-famous community, a struggle for power develops among the longtime prioress, the saint, and the Duke's daughter. After much tribulation and the saint's election as prioress, a secret denunciation to the Inquisition brings the narrator and the saint to trial. Following months of inquiry and confinement for the two women, both are convicted. The saint is ordered into isolation for several years at a different convent, while the narrator's sentence consists of moderate acts of contrition and penitence. Before the saint can carry out her sentence, however, the infection caused by the wounds in her hands spreads throughout her body, and she dies amid the squalid conditions of her convent.

The reliance on a first-person narrator as mediating consciousness of *Outside the Walls* presents clear advantages and disadvantages, both for revealing the principal psychological conflicts and for the development of style and technique. In the first place, the use of the nun (i.e., a character who forms part of the specific spatial and temporal setting) enables Fernández Santos to employ a kind of language that coincides with and enhances the seventeenth-century ambience. Since the nun "lives" during the seventeenth century, her narration naturally and fluidly employs the language of the time. Although the novelist has modernized her vocabulary and style to make it more accessible to the contemporary reader (one critic suggests that the language is more "unusual" than properly seventeenth century),[7] it nonetheless contributes to historical verisimilitude. At the same time, it permits the insertion of pseudomystical language into the natural flow of the discourse. The narrator frequently reflects on her love for the saint, explaining their relationship with spiritual language similar to that of the sixteenth-century Spanish mystics.

Nothing in the novel suggests that the nun is less than reliable in her role as narrator. She appears as a trustworthy conveyor of both external phenomena and internal conflict, and her views are not undermined by contradiction or deceit. Although the novel primarily consists of her recollections, she does not break conventional patterns of time and space. The narrative develops chronologically, free of temporal fragmentation, following sequentially the flow of events. On occasion, however, the narrator employs a temporal prolepsis, which functions primarily on two levels. First, it reminds the reader that the narrative present represents the past for the narrator as she retells her story. Second, it creates tension and the expectation of impending tragedy. Such is the case, for example, when the narrator and the saint search for ways to obtain food and money for the convent. The narrator remarks that something has occurred "that I will relate later,"[8] and this unnamed event perhaps "[initiated] the ruin of all of us, of our honorable name and reputation" (16). Hence from the outset the narrator hints at a tragedy that has already taken place, but within the chronological flow of the narrative it must await its proper sequential appearance.

Several obvious limitations accompany the use of a restricted point of view in *Outside the Walls*. The most important of these relates specifically to the portrayal of the two nuns. Although we are invited to probe the narrator's thoughts and conflicts throughout the novel, we learn very little about the mental processes of the saint. For the most part, her character emerges only in relation to the needs, desires, and fears of the narrator, and therefore has no existence independent of the observing "I." We never discover her true feelings toward the narrator, nor can we be certain if she comes to believe in the miraculous powers of her own hands. Perhaps even more importantly, she is isolated from the narrator for several months during their trial. Since the narrator never provides privileged information that could only be known by an omniscient observer, a large gap exists in the saint's character portrayal.[9] Hence the saint remains an ambiguous figure, even though she constantly occupies the meditations of the narrator and plays a central role in the development of plot.

Outside the Walls circumvents moral judgment concerning the amorous relationship of the two nuns, although within the context of seventeenth-century Spain homosexuality most often led to trial and execution by the Inquisition. To a large extent, of course, the moral implications of lesbianism can only be examined by the narrator. Since she questions neither the rightness of her desires nor the loftiness of her feelings, the moral dilemma never arises. This is not to say, however, that she does not reflect upon her actions and motivations. On the contrary, she is obsessed with her love for the saint to such an extent that it constantly occupies her thoughts and shapes her view of life. For the most part, she seeks to ennoble their love and articulates her emotions in a spiritual-mystical language that echoes the writing of Santa Teresa de Jesús and San Juan de la Cruz. Indeed, the narrator frequently draws upon the identical sensual imagery to express her carnal desire that Spanish mystics used to define their spiritual union with God. For example:

My soul, overwhelmed by love, searched for its habitual medicine, the principal means of elevating it above the other terrestrial loves, in the warm refuge of her arms. Nothing stopped me this time, no net or door hindered me. My flesh was no longer a burdensome weight, but rather the light wing of a bird in search of a nest in which to sow caresses and tenderness. Body and soul were united, and regaled one another in a secret game that . . . elevated and united us for life. Then came a quiet, tranquil peace, a repose of body, an awakening of the soul like that which one must feel in heaven. (110−11)

They are right when they say that Christ loved us, and if we don't imitate Him we are not like Him, not in our actions or our countenance, but rather we are poor, blind, and mute, because only love makes man live. Let us love each other, then, my sister, more than any other well-being or benefit, let us love one another, and we will be like God; let us suffer our anxious solitude together, let us suffer in each other. (161−62)

Only by placing the narrator's language in the context of her physical desires is it discernible from genuinely mystical speech patterns. Carnal passion clearly motivates the relationship between the two women—the narrator even admits that she is "a slave of love" (60)—but the narrator consistently seeks to elevate this passion to a divine plane. She remains convinced throughout the novel of the virtue of her love, not in the eyes of the other nuns but certainly in the eyes of God: "I never considered it a sin to love the Holy Creator through His creatures, nor did I consider that I, a poor servant, was capable of failing Him in anything. . . . Once our will has been surrendered to God, how can temptations be resisted? In perpetual prayer, how can one offend Him, since love among His creatures is holier than the other virtues?" (85−86).[10]

While the narrator's moral justification for her love affair with the saint remains constant, her participation in the "miracle" of the hands spawns indecision and fear. She admits that the miracle has aided the convent and produced a new spirit of hope. As conditions improve for the community she even doubts if any deception has occurred at all, and grants that the wounds may truly represent a sign of God's favor. But the saint's increasing power and fame, coupled with her frequent manifestations of vanity and pride, create a growing schism between the two women. Furthermore, her abstract theological declarations concerning the "miracle" confuse the narrator and intensify her apprehension. Eventually the narrator recognizes that their personal intimacy has been subordinated to the saint's lofty aspirations. She feels abandoned and isolated, and proclaims her complete insignificance when compared

with the more noble status of her lover: "As far as the world is concerned, I am dust, nothing less than [the saint's] shadow" (191). The
narrator's continual vacillation between loyalty to the saint on the one
hand and her fear of God's punishment for her role in the saint's wounds
on the other arouses such conflicting emotions within her that she often
feels compelled to confess her guilt publicly. Her subservient role comes
clearly into focus on these occasions, however. The saint placates her
with a night of ardent love, and the narrator's loyalty is reaffirmed.

More than in any other of Fernández Santos's novels the narrative of
Outside the Walls is dominated by a single character, whose conflicts,
emotions, and doubts emerge as the work progresses. As previously
pointed out, this process of self-revelation remains generally free of
distortions and deceptions. More important in terms of self-characteri-
zation, however, the progression of the narrative does not represent a
movement from blindness to insight. The narrator never reaches a
crucial moment of self-recognition in which she suddenly gains new
perceptions into her own psyche or that of the saint. Her rational and
firm hold on reality, although punctuated with moments of doubt and
emotion, is maintained throughout the course of her recollections. This
is perhaps best exemplified in the portrayal of the two principal plot lines
of the novel, the love affair and the false wounds. From the outset the
narrator views the saint's deception as fraudulent and sinful, but consistently affirms the rightness of her love for the saint. Even when she
faces trial by the Holy Tribunal it never occurs to the narrator that her
lesbian affair, if discovered, could bring about her execution. From her
own perspective, her sin is manifest in the wounds in the saint's hands,
not in the carnal desires that hold her captive: "They haven't said
anything to me about the matter of the wounds, the only thing for which
in truth and according to my memory they could denounce and condemn
me" (201). The narrator does not attempt to conceal her love for the
saint; it simply does not represent cause for contrition.

Another integral aspect of the narrator's psyche that emerges from her
recollections centers on the purpose and function of God in a divinely
ordered world. Despite the ascetic doctrine that demands abstinence and
self-sacrifice in order to gain eternal salvation, the narrator fails to
reconcile the human misery surrounding her with the notion of a
benevolent and loving God. She is unable to comprehend, for example,
how suffering enhances one's eternal glory; whether the severe drought is
the work of God or of Satan; or what the poor people of the villages have
done to offend God so as to deserve such harsh punishment. She does not
strive to resolve this conflict through abstract or profoundly theological

reflection, for the nature of her religious devotion is never confused with intellectual meditation. The narrator does not envisage herself as a victim of supernatural or cosmic forces, but simply expresses her grief over the tragic state of her immediate circumstances. In the end, of course, she accedes to the prevailing doctrines that seek to explain these contradictions as the will of God.

Despite the narrator's bewilderment concerning theological conflict, or the persistent fears and isolation that afflict her, she expresses no sentiments of alienation. Even during the trial and separation from the saint, and later following the saint's death, her faith in God's ultimate benevolence remains firm. In direct contrast to the existential dilemmas of characters in Fernández Santos's previous works, the narrator of *Outside the Walls* does not doubt the stability of a divinely ordered cosmos or her role within it. Whereas Amparo of *The Untamed*, Margarita of *The Book of Memorable Events*, or Miguel of *In the Fire* are oppressed by the nothingness of their existence, the narrator of *Outside the Walls* constantly affirms her trust in God even as the world crumbles about her. Hence while there exists a profoundly Baroque sense of disillusionment and conflict both within and outside the convent, the narrator ultimately achieves tranquility via the integration of earthly and divine love, as is explicitly revealed in her entreaty to God at the end of the novel. She despairs over the physical death of the saint ("It is my life that I defend in her, my salvation that lies in her hands, my destiny and reason for being that is born and dies in her, in her body in times of victory, a body that today is empty and dead, cause of nothingness" [252]), but again incorporates her love into the divine realm of grace and salvation: "When, Lord, will our long-promised time of glory come? Here we are, the two of us clinging to your love that is able to save us, able to change wretched pain into happiness, able to show us the road that leads to you like a flame of joy growing toward the clouds" (253).

In nearly all of his novels Fernández Santos has forged a specific physical and historical milieu that is powerfully wrought and meticulously drawn. Most frequently, the atmosphere of his novels is rooted in isolation and ruin. Such is the case, for example, with the small town of postwar Spain portrayed in *The Untamed* or the mountain village of Asturias depicted in *The One Who Has No Name*. The creation of milieu in *Outside the Walls* follows a similar pattern, and Fernández Santos draws upon historical circumstance to heighten its authenticity and impact. The conditions of seventeenth-century Spain include some of the most devastating in the country's history. By the mid-1590s the revenue-producing capacities of Spain were reaching their limit. Already heavy

taxes were increased and essential foodstuffs were burdened with particularly harsh tariffs. Agriculture languished and the economy slumped
dramatically during the last part of the sixteenth century and beginning
of the seventeenth. Harvests failed, prices rose, and the Spanish masses
suffered hunger and economic hardship. The plague also devastated
Spain near the end of the 1590s, and as much as 25 percent of the
population died from the disease.[11]

Fernández Santos integrates the essence of these historical circumstances into the novel, but maintains ambiguity by omitting place-
names and dates. Within the historical parameters the portrayal of life at
the convent in many ways offers a microcosmic view of the times as a
whole. As occurs in several of Fernández Santos's previous works, much
of the character portrayal turns upon the commingling of climatic
conditions, physical decay, and a pervasive desolation that abrogates
human existence. To a large degree, therefore, the narrative focuses on
the complete physical ruin of the convent and its surroundings. In
descriptive fragments recalling passages from several of Fernández
Santos's earlier novels, the narrator underscores the squalid living conditions by repeatedly using the word "ruin" (e.g., pp. 8, 10, 13, 34, etc.).
Scant food is available for the nuns because the area has been devastated
by drought, and the stark physical appearance of the landscape reifies the
sense of doom that consumes the collective psyche. As the narrator
observes, "The area used to be fertile and filled with various sorts
of people, with water wheels and orchards, churches and hospitals.
Nothing remains of all that, only dried, hard mud and a random
animal half-eaten by flies that, in this blind world, are encamped
like lords in their fief. Everything around, sky and fields and streams,
proclaims death, leaves one's spirit contrite, drying out our insides . . ."
(66–67). In addition, most of the people from the nearby villages have
fled into the hills in hope of escaping the plague. Within the convent,
nuns die of starvation and disease, and even their faith fails to mitigate
the overwhelming sense of fatalism. Outside the convent there is little
faith and no hope among the masses. In short, Fernández Santos portrays
Spain as a country in the midst of religious, economic, and social
turmoil. As a consequence, he is able to offer the most direct social
criticism of any of his novels to date.

For the most part, the social focus of *Outside the Walls* underscores the
unjust treatment of the poor by the rich. Spanish society during the
seventeenth century consisted mainly of two classes (the rich and the
poor) and, as J. H. Elliott has shown, "the criterion for distinguishing
between them lay not in their rank or social position, but in whether

they had anything to eat."[12] Fernández Santos draws sharp distinctions between the two classes through both direct and indirect social commentary. The implied criticism takes the form of motifs that recur in relation to the convent and the townspeople. For example, the drought deprives the masses of food; water at the convent grows stagnant; the nuns receive no offerings of help because the local residents have nothing to give. A constant pattern of desolation and gloom among the poor runs throughout the novel, and its thematic impact is heightened through contrast with the upper class.

The disparity between classes is most strikingly conveyed by the Duke and his daughter, who display the contemptuous demeanor of wealth and power. The two royal figures represent perhaps the flattest characters of any of Fernández Santos's novels, and stand in pronounced opposition to the poverty of the nuns and villagers. For example, when the daughter resides at the convent she wears magnificent clothing and is attended by her private servant. The Duke's arrival at the convent "[filled] the road with shining arms, covering hills and nearby walls like we had never seen before. It seemed as if the King Our Lord himself had arrived with all his majesty, that the entire court with its ministers and advisers traveled surrounding him" (123). The narrator, however, uniquely debases the Duke's entourage through a form of bathetic vitiation. The caravan appears to the narrator "like the worms in the orchard" (123) as it progresses along the road in the distance. The debasement suggested by the simile is clear, although it fits smoothly into the narrative flow so as to suggest that the narrator herself is unaware of the acuteness of her observation.

The other form of social criticism is voiced directly by secondary characters rather than conveyed by the narrator or implied by the action. For example, the gardener appears twice in the novel, and on each occasion he condemns the exploitation of the poor. When driving the narrator to visit her sick father, the gardener reflects on the present conditions of society: "He who works . . . has to support himself and the owner of the property and the revenue collector and the tax collector, because prelates, nobles, and lords, those who hoard the grain that the rest of us plant, don't pay anything; they only receive what others work for. They don't pay duties because they put that weight on our backs" (128). When he later appears near the end of the novel, he again denounces social injustice: "In any case . . . , such is life; some out of fear, others out of petty interests, everyone tries to bury the weakest, while the powerful, amid papal bulls and duties, prosper, year after year, and still presume to be merciful" (242). The Duke clearly exemplifies this rich/poor dichotomy, most poignantly when he denigrates the peasants who refuse to pay their taxes. He ruthlessly persecutes the rebellious farmers, viewing his subjects as "miserable laborers" (128). Even though the farmers have defied the laws of the Royal Court simply in order to survive (i.e., they have no food or money to offer the king), the Duke condemns their actions and is intent on their punishment.

The Inquisition is also expressly condemned in the novel. In contrast to the absence of moralization concerning the love between the two nuns, a moral position clearly emerges in relation to the Inquisition and its administration of justice. The powers of the Inquisition during the late sixteenth and early seventeenth century became so absolute that thousands of persons were prosecuted because of secret denunciations against them. Fernández Santos exposes the arbitrary justice of the Holy Tribunal both through the principal and secondary characters. For example, the two nuns are isolated in miserable cells for several months without trial, and they never discover who has accused them. The narrator's jailer also has suffered the inequities of Church justice, and lost his family and wealth after being falsely accused of heresy. The jailer not only assails the work of the Holy Tribunal, but also voices the Baroque disillusionment that it has helped create. As he explains to the narrator: "The worst part about this world is being summoned into it, to come into it with the hope of being happy. They bring us here and then abandon us here, and here we dance until the Final Judgment according to the tune that comes from above" (222). From the secret denunciations that sustained it, to the wretched conditions in its overcrowded jails, the Inquisition is portrayed in *Outside the Walls* as a pervasive agent of terror. Not only did it humiliate innocent victims, but it brought shame to their families, destroyed their lives, and helped undermine the stability of Spanish society.

Outside the Walls does not represent for Fernández Santos a break with his previous fiction, but rather reaffirms his interest in re-creating and exploring the historical past through a specific fictional mode. In addition, it continues the evolution initiated in *The Man of the Saints* toward the probing of an individual, rather than collective, psyche, although the technique of self-revelation through first-person narration is unique to *Outside the Walls*. As in all of his previous novels, Fernández Santos places the characters of *Outside the Walls* in a well-defined milieu. The specific social and physical atmosphere of seventeenth-century Spain, as well as the desolate and solitary existence within the convent, to a large degree enclose and determine the lives of the two nuns. This pseudodeterministic commingling of character and environment shapes much of Fernández Santos's early fiction and continues to function as one of the principal elements of his narrative. Fernández Santos also remains socially engaged in *Outside the Walls* (i.e., he continues to utilize the literary work as a medium for social commentary), although the constructs used to convey his commitment and the literary milieu that results stand in sharp opposition to his earlier works of Social Realism. In sum, *Outside the Walls* adheres in many ways to the norms of Fernández Santos's past fiction but also offers new modes of expression through the diversification of language and technique, and its unique thematic focus on lesbianism in a seventeenth-century Spanish convent.

Cabrera

Fernández Santos's continuing interest in re-creating the Spanish past in his fiction provides the basic framework for *Cabrera*, first published in the fall of 1981. In contrast to *The One Who Has No Name* and *Outside the Walls*, which are set ambiguously in medieval and Renaissance Spain, *Cabrera* takes place during a specific time period, 1808–1814, and recounts concrete events from the Napoleonic invasion of Spain. To a large degree, therefore, historical circumstance frames the narrative of *Cabrera* and also helps to shape its thematic focus. That is to say, the novel is cast in such a way that its referential system is rooted firmly in Spanish history of the early nineteenth century, and against this backdrop a series of fictional characters incarnate both historical and individual conflicts. More specifically, Fernández Santos focuses on a unique aspect of Spanish history as reported through the eyes of his fictional narrator: life in the first modern concentration camp, constructed in 1809 on the Balearic island of Cabrera.[13] The novel thus develops as a personal account of the war and its impact on the young narrator, whose plight is tied intimately both to the nature of the conflict and the uncertainty of its outcome.

The historical focus of the novel centers for the most part on the isle of Cabrera, to which several thousand French soldiers and Spaniards sympathetic to their cause were transported following the Battle of Bailén in 1808. The fictitious narrator/protagonist relates events leading up to the battle in the first part of the novel, but the principal emphasis lies with the concentration camp itself. According to historical records (to which *Cabrera* adheres closely), in May of 1808 a French army marched south from Toledo in order to secure the port of Cádiz. The column consisted of several thousand soldiers (both French regulars and foreign mercenaries) and a large contingent of Spanish civilians, who worked for the French or simply followed the column seeking economic gain. The column progressed easily during the early days of its march, and not until Córdoba did it encounter an ill-equipped Spanish army. After quickly disposing of the Spanish resistance, the French soldiers pillaged Córdoba and destroyed many of its valuable art treasures. A few weeks later, however, the French army was defeated at the Battle of Bailén, and many of the soldiers and their civilian entourage became prisoners of war. Taken first to Cádiz, where thousands died in unsanitary and cramped quarters, the approximately five thousand survivors of the column were finally transported to Cabrera in the spring of 1809.[14]

According to firsthand accounts,[15] life on Cabrera was quickly reduced to survival at the lowest level of human existence. Housing was not provided for the prisoners, and thus they were forced to live in caves or construct small huts. The prisoners were scarcely able to protect themselves from the cold and rain during the winter, and many men had no clothing whatsoever. Food had to be sent to the island by boat, but inclement weather often delayed shipments for weeks at a time. Indeed, food became so scarce that cannibalism was reported on several occasions. The island itself was nearly bare of vegetation, with no reliable supply of water, and disease and starvation plagued the camp during the five years of its existence. Of the nearly sixteen thousand prisoners sent to Cabrera from 1809 to 1813, approximately three thousand survived.[16]

By relating certain historical events of the Napoleonic invasion, the narrator provides a concrete framework within which to tell his story and to develop the principal thematic concerns of the novel. On the one hand, Cabrera conveys the narrator's personal struggle to survive in a society that has shunned him since birth. Similar to many of Fernández Santos's post—social-realistic novels, Cabrera focuses on the individual character adrift in a world that remains indifferent to his predicament. Beyond this, however, the novel portrays the larger historical conflict between Spain and France, and the civil strife and divisiveness to which it leads. Cabrera thus advances two parallel stories, each dependent upon the other for the development of plot as well as for the elucidation of theme.

Both the narrative structure and content of Cabrera create the initial impression that the novel coincides with the picaresque tradition in Spanish literature. For example, the young narrator sets out in the world first in order to survive, then to transcend the limits of his social class. He relates his uncertain lineage, his early years spent at an orphanage, and how he finally escaped the orphanage by agreeing to work on a farm. The priest at the orphanage is described in typical picaresque fashion as corrupt and greedy, one who deprives the children of food donated to support them. The narrator admits to a passion for wine (reminiscent of Lazarillo de Tormes), and as he leaves the orphanage he already conspires to abandon his new master and seek his fortune in the world. There is also in the early sections of the novel an undertone of cynicism in the narrator's views, a wisdom beyond his years forged from the hardships of the orphanage. Finally, in a leitmotiv that recurs throughout the novel, the traditional picaresque theme of hunger determines many of the narrator's actions and helps to shape his view of the world.

With the exception of these superficial points of contact, however, *Cabrera* transcends the limiting generic traditions of the picaresque in its thematic vision and portrayal of character. Although both of these aspects of the novel will be discussed later in detail, one other essential element sets the work apart from the picaresque—the tone that marks the narrator's tale. To be sure, *Cabrera* is (like the picaresque) both the story of a human life and a commentary on the system of values in which human lives are framed. Unlike the picaresque, however, in which there is an unchanging emphasis on the corruption of society,[17] the narrative world of *Cabrera* turns to a large degree upon the meditations of a narrator attempting to comprehend life at a variety of levels: political, historical, physical, spiritual. Rather than exploit society by cynical and selfish deceptions, the narrator seeks instead a more basic existential freedom in which he can be "alone, prosperous and free."[18] In this sense, *Cabrera* becomes a novel of ideas about the nature of life, both in its crudest form of physical subsistence and in its more complex system of human ideals. In the end, the narrator remains on the fringes of society as a victim of its cruelty. But the philosophical view that he develops and the historical forces that shape this development clearly distinguish him from the traditional picaresque hero.

The two principal thematic preoccupations of the novel—the horror of war and survival of the protagonist—are of course made available to the reader solely as they emerge from the consciousness of the narrator. Despite the marked spatial and temporal variations (e.g., the march of the French army through southern Spain, the five-year imprisonment on Cabrera), these themes remain constant even as the narrator experiences the world in diverse situations and encounters a broad range of people. That is to say, the narrative is marked from the beginning by a *Weltan-schauung* that is reinforced, rather than transformed, by the narrator's experiences outside the confines of the orphanage. What gives thematic intensity to the novel, therefore, is that the views of other characters counterposed to those of the narrator are eventually undermined by the destructive social and historical forces that control the characters' destinies. Hence, rather than function as an initiation story, as does much of Fernández Santos's fiction about Spanish youths,[19] *Cabrera* conveys an axiological perspective that is shaped by poverty early in the narrator's life, and affirmed through time by the nature of society itself.

The narrator's response to the prevailing historical forces (the French invasion and the devastation that it causes) is implicit in all that he relates. Apart from his role as pseudohistorical voice (i.e., as conveyer of facts about the invasion), the narrator is important because of his ideas about these facts, and because his life to a large degree depends upon the way in which they evolve. Despite his young age when he joins the French column, the narrator quickly develops an attitude toward the war in which nobility of purpose plays no part. His view is not that of a child too young to understand historical conflict, but rather of a boy compelled to sustain himself amid hostility and death: "The rest [of the war] hardly mattered to me: the atrocities committed by the troops; the ambushes by the Spaniards; the bodies that remained behind. . . . I was my own person. My country, my age, began and ended within the shadow of my blanket" (27). That is to say, he consistently seeks to deny the historical circumstances that shape his existence at the same time that he is forced to adapt to them. He travels with the French column not as a gesture of support for their cause, but as a way of improving his lot. He quickly discovers that political ideology serves little purpose—"All that matters in war is choosing the side that wins" (32)—and he would willingly abandon the column (as he does for a short time to serve a wealthy family) if his future seemed more prosperous elsewhere. It must be understood, however, that what defines and impels this view of the world does not emerge in the novel as amoral or immoral delinquency. Indeed, the self-conscious meditations of the narrator are never hardened by cynicism or corrupted by false pretense. On the contrary, his ideas and actions grow from a more fundamental level of physical sustenance, and his most profound pronouncements on the war are made from this perspective. As he watches one of his starving friends attack a companion, he remarks that "I understand how war and misery are capable of changing a person, all for a crust of bread which, years ago, not even a dog would eat" (143).

The narrator's view of the world in many ways corresponds with that of several of Fernández Santos's earlier protagonists—for example, Antonio of *The Man of the Saints*, Miguel of *In the Fire*, or Margarita of *The Book of Memorable Events*. All of these characters are skeptical of inherent meaning in life, and all suffer profound existential anguish as a result.

Furthermore, each proceeds through life amid isolation and solitude, and each finds that a resolution to his dilemma remains beyond reach. In contrast to these characters, however, the narrator of *Cabrera*, while accepting the burden of daily survival, looks to the future as if his life were guided by the powerful forces of Destiny. For example, when the narrator flees his first master in order to join the French column, the impetus for doing so comes from without: "Destiny, which with a single stroke resolves so often the doubts of men, pushed me among carts and arms carriers, horsemen and soldiers"(20). Later, when asked to participate in covert political activity for the French, the narrator notes that "I remain silent, waiting like I have so often for fortune to decide for me" (79). Throughout the novel the strategy of the narrator is "to put himself in the hands of Fortune" (33), and to move through life with scant hope that his fortune will improve. Indeed, what he learns through experience is that, "fortune favors you only to turn around and become scornful" (91).

The future of the narrator, then, is shaped both by historical circumstance and by the undefined forces of Destiny. The pseudodeterministic atmosphere that characterizes much of Fernández Santos's earlier fiction also functions in *Cabrera*, in this instance to preclude the narrator from forging his own fate. He is bound to the misfortunes of his birth, despite repeated attempts to transcend them, and he gradually recognizes that his hope of being "alone, prosperous and free" is a mere fantasy. Although he accepts his destiny with a certain stoicism, he comes to represent perhaps the most vanquished of Fernández Santos's characters: "I know nothing and nothing matters. Only that I remain enchained, dependent upon others to decide for me. My destiny is to be silent, obey, not rebel, and to know that, beyond any doubt, I will never free myself from this chain that has accompanied me since I was born . . ." (246).

A fundamentally opposing view of the world is conveyed in the novel by one of the narrator's companions, known simply as *el amigo* ("the friend"). The narrator becomes acquainted with his friend shortly after joining the column, but recognizes immediately their difference in social class and education. The friend speaks French as well as Spanish, and there is about him an air of wealth and dignity. He is less concerned with daily survival than the narrator and passes nearly all of his time with the French soldiers. Beyond these superficial differences, however, the friend articulates a romantic view of war that contrasts sharply with the more practical concerns voiced by the narrator. In the first place, the friend is an *afrancesado* ("supporter of the French"), and thus actively involves himself in the historical conflict taking place around him. This stands in direct opposition to the apolitical stance of the narrator, who remains aloof from the ideological controversy of the war. More importantly, however, the friend repeatedly insists upon the nobility of war and the honor of the French army, even as civilians are slaughtered and soldiers imprisoned amid inhuman conditions: "War is a noble profession, as long as its rules are respected" (41).

The views of the friend are also enhanced by the letters written between him and his father and intercalated into the narrative at various points. The father is a professional soldier serving in the Spanish army in France, and through him the son envisions war as an ennobling activity characterized by dignity and fair play. The tone of the father's early letters clearly supports this belief; hence the friend survives his miserable existence with the French column by clinging to the hope of a glorious future in which he too will become a soldier. As the novel progresses, however, the idealism articulated by the son (and implied by the father in his letters) becomes increasingly vitiated. Significantly, this unraveling of their ideals does not originate from without, but rather emerges specifically from within their system of values and experiences. For the son, the process of change is a gradual one that begins with the defeat of the French at Bailén and intensifies amid the dehumanizing conditions of his imprisonment on Cabrera. Only when he learns that Napoleon has been defeated, however (and, ironically, that he will be set free), does he recognize the futility of his dreams.

The father's process of disillusion runs a parallel course, and is linked with equal poignancy to the disastrous events of the war in eastern Europe. As his regiment becomes more directly involved in Napoleon's military campaign, the father witnesses the degradation of soldiers forced to work like prisoners: "Our soldiers are used to repair roads and fortifications, and rather than military men, we seem more like prisoners of war. All of this is done to reduce expenses. . . . There is a good number of Spanish prisoners here. They don't bear arms; their task is not that much different from ours . . ." (138–39). In addition, the violent death and absurdity of the fighting inspire doubt and fear as the army penetrates deeper into Russia. The father's final letter to his son suggests his imminent death, and, rather than end his life with the "miserable glory" (89) of the battlefield, the father desires an "honorable peace" (89) that will end the tragedy of the war.

It is also by means of the letters between father and son that the historical theme of "two Spains" is developed most explicitly. From the middle of the eighteenth century, when French culture (through the ruling Bourbons) became deeply entrenched in Spanish society, the conflict between it and Spain's traditional cultural and religious values grew increasingly more acute. The *afrancesados* and many Spanish liberals embraced the opening of Spain to European ideas, while the Church and conservative groups resisted European influence and sought to sustain traditional Spanish institutions. The friend's father expresses ambivalence concerning this conflict ("It will be difficult to choose, without our honor suffering, between serving the new King José and defending our beloved independence" [56]), but the son clearly supports the liberal demand for change: "I have met new people, men prepared not to let this opportunity to change the destiny of our country escape, to save it from its misery and its ignorance. We are all fighting to spread the spirit of the new King José, but it is not easy to convince these stubborn Spaniards" (83). For the most part, however, this controversy remains unresolved in the novel, since Fernández Santos concerns himself less with the development of history than with the portrayal of character.

Several additional characters form part of the narrator's tale, the most important of which are the chaplain sent to the island of Cabrera, and a friend known simply as *el cojo* ("the cripple"). For the most part, *el cojo* serves to complement the life and attitudes of the narrator. He too must scavenge for his daily ration of food and learns to survive without committing himself to the French cause. Similar to the narrator, in fact, his sole commitment is to himself. His country is "the world" (58) and he will journey "wherever my feet take me" (58). He also coincides with the narrator in his rejection of the friend's view of war. When the friend expounds upon the virtues of fighting and dying with honor, and lauds the noble codes of war, *el cojo* responds with a cynicism that reflects his miserable circumstances: "I wouldn't give half a swig of wine for it" (196); and later, "'What is [the art of war]? The Swiss fighting for whomever pays them the most; others for booty, beginning with the generals. . . . Look at them; there they are'—he pointed to the mounds of earth crowned with crosses. 'In life they only knew how to fight, die, conquer or be conquered. Where is their honor, their glory?'" (234). In short, although his character is less fully developed than that of the friend, *el cojo* clearly enhances theme through his echoing of the narrator's sentiments and through his daily struggle to survive.

The chaplain is by far the most complexly portrayed of the peripheral characters in the novel. On the one hand, he incarnates the spirit of charity and sacrifice through his work with the prisoners. He succeeds in building a crude hospital on the island and pleads with the authorities to supply the prisoners with food and clothing. At the same time, however, he is tormented by private demons that divert him from pastoral goodness. It becomes clear by the end of the novel that the priest has been exiled to Cabrera for his illicit sexual conduct in the past. Despite his current efforts to combat his carnal desires—for example, he orders that all women be sent to the mainland—he again succumbs to temptation. Ironically, perhaps the only act of true charity in the narrator's life precipitates the priest's demise. When the narrator faces harsh punishment following an attempted escape, María (a young girl he has been hiding from the authorities) offers herself to the priest in order to protect the narrator. After exploiting the girl as his personal concubine, the priest abandons her to the prisoners, who attack and kill her shortly before their release. Similar to the narrator at the end of the novel, the priest reflects upon "his sad destiny" (230) and looks toward a future that will, like the narrator's, parallel the misery of the past: "Amid all his valor and sacrifice there only remains the certainty that life will remain the same; he will never attain the peace that he hopes for" (231).

Several other characters move in and out of the novel during the course of the narrator's tale. Fernández Santos is generally careful to avoid stereotypes, but these characters frequently come to embody certain aspects of turn-of-the-century Spanish society. For example, while many aristocrats praise the new French government and the progress it will bring to Spain, others argue for Spanish independence. French mercenaries ransack the countryside, while independent Spaniards exploit the prisoners of Cabrera. A young woman with scant political awareness lives a solitary life while the man she is to marry fights for Spanish autonomy; Spanish peasants resist the French in prolonged guerrilla warfare. Although none of these characters forms a crucial part of either plot or theme, viewed as a whole they serve to enhance the realistic milieu of the novel. They represent a wide range of people encountered by the narrator and make his story rounded and complete.

In sum, *Cabrera* does not diverge greatly from the path of writing fictional history that has marked Fernández Santos's narrative since *The One Who Has No Name*. Similar to his novels of the late 1970s, Fernández Santos establishes a historical and social reality in *Cabrera* that helps to shape the characters' lives and determine their actions. Most importantly, the recurrent influence of the war forms a leitmotiv throughout the novel, and Fernández Santos draws the conflict in such a way that the narrator is unable to escape its misery and destruction. Also similar to much of his recent fiction, *Cabrera* focuses on the dilemma of an individual character, rather than creating a collective protagonist. The narrator of *Cabrera* emerges as a tragic figure not only because he suffers from hunger and poverty, but also because he is permitted scant hope of transcending his circumstances. In this regard, *Cabrera* coincides with nearly all of Fernández Santos's fiction, in which the characters are submerged in an abulic and destructive atmosphere from which they cannot hope to escape. Although the narrator of *Cabrera* at one time dreams of wealth and comfort ("My furtive dreams were soaring and I saw myself as an admiral or cardenal, a captain or servant of the Eternal Father" [11−12]), his illusions gradually yield to the grimmer realities of his daily life: "My former illusions seemed very far away now" (65).

Although *Cabrera* became a best-selling novel in Spain in late 1981, it was not received with the same popular and critical enthusiasm awarded *Outside the Walls*, Fernández Santos's previous novel. Nonetheless, *Cabrera* forms an important part of Fernández Santos's still-evolving narrative scheme. It reaffirms the author's commitment to creating a literature of imagination that reflects Spain's distant past, yet does not imply a radical break with the fundamental traits of his earlier fiction. In terms of style and technique, *Cabrera* is perhaps the least complex of Fernández Santos's recent novels. It offers a straightforward first-person narration related in chronological order, and only the interpolated letters of the friend's father interrupt the single narrative perspective. Yet the direct rendering of the tale in no way detracts from its interest. Indeed, *Cabrera* is successful to a large degree because of Fernández Santos's extraordinary ability to tell a good story and to draw complex characters that incarnate both individual and universal problems. This has become a recurring trait of Fernández Santos's best fiction, and it has made him one of the most respected novelists of postwar Spain.

Chapter Five
Short Fiction

Fernández Santos has observed on several occasions that he regards himself more as a novelist than a writer of short stories. He also maintains that he most frequently writes short narrative in order to practice a technique or develop an idea that he intends to expand later into a longer narrative.[1] While both of these views overlook the literary merit of Fernández Santos's stories, as well as their role in helping to revitalize short fiction in Spain during the past two decades, they are in general perceptive and accurate. Fernández Santos's reputation as a writer indeed stems primarily from his novels, while his collections of short stories generally foreshadow or coincide with the different stages of his novelistic evolution. *Cabeza rapada* [Shaved Head, 1958], for example, which contains stories written as early as 1950, manifests many of the thematic concerns and technical constructs characterizing the author's neo-realistic novels. The collections *Las catedrales* [The Cathedrals, 1970] and *Paraíso encerrado* [Enclosed Paradise, 1973] offer the religious backdrop and temporal fragmentation more fully developed in *The Man of the Saints* and *The Book of Memorable Events*, and foreshadow the cycle of historical re-creation and legend that forms the nucleus of *The One Who Has No Name* and *Outside the Walls*. However, *A orillas de una vieja dama* [Within Sight of an Old Lady, 1979], Fernández Santos's most recent collection of short narrative, seemingly interrupts this pattern of parallel development. Both the methodological and thematic diversity of its stories would appear to preclude a close correspondence with the author's novelistic evolution.

For more than a century writers and literary critics have debated what precisely constitutes a modern short story. From Poe's restrictive precepts defining length and scope, to the broader outlines offered by later theorists, none of the explanations, as H. E. Bates observes, "defines the short story with an indisputable epigrammatic accuracy which will fit all short stories."[2] Fernández Santos himself has not theorized on the short story, nor has he attempted to narrow its limits by formulating a restrictive generic definition. Indeed, a perusal of his stories clearly points to broad parameters in length, theme, and technique. His shortest narratives consist of only a few pages, while the longest span up to eighty pages. Narrative point of view also varies widely among the stories, while structural patterns and stylistic elements reflect the multifarious transformations that have marked Fernández Santos's literary evolution as a whole. H. E. Bates concludes in his overview of short fiction that the short story "is anything that the author decides it shall be."[3] This open-ended interpretation aptly defines the short narrative of Fernández Santos, who views generic distinctions as neither problematic nor controversial.

Cabeza rapada

In *Cabeza rapada* [Shaved Head], Fernández Santos brings together several short stories published previously in literary magazines of the early 1950s. The fourteen stories that compose the collection represent in many ways a compendium of the principal thematic and technical elements found in Fernández Santos's early fiction. The devastating consequences of war, children's perspectives on their surroundings, and the portrayal of abulia and nothingness constitute the three principal thematic concerns of the stories and provide a continuity of tone marked by grief and despair. Several stories contain biographical elements from Fernández Santos's youth (especially those that relate childhood experiences of the Civil War), while others offer a microcosmic view of the misery and poverty of small-town life that forms the nucleus of *The Untamed* and *In the Fire*.

The immediacy of the Civil War, as well as the general sense of fear and destruction caused by the fighting, is felt more acutely in these stories than in Fernández Santos's early novels. The writer treats war both from the viewpoint of adults, who participate in it, and from the perspective of young children, old enough to sense danger and experience fear, but who do not fully comprehend the devastating horror. Two of the stories, "El sargento" [The Sergeant] and "El final de una guerra" [The End of a War], convey the destructive and unheroic realities of war. In the former, a sergeant based in Cuba during the Spanish American War aspires to become involved in combat to fulfill his fantasies of heroism. Instead, he is charged with overseeing the burial of scores of soldiers who die daily from wounds and disease. During the course of the story the narrator/sergeant offers a detailed and grotesque accounting of the effects of malaria and the agonizing death that it causes. The sergeant's constant mental anguish is mitigated only by the hope of winning glory on the battlefield. Before he is able to return to the fighting, however, he is stricken with malaria, and amid delirium and pain he dies without heroism in the hospital.

A similar view of unheroic death is portrayed in "The End of a War." As two young deserters cautiously make their way to Madrid, they are captured and imprisoned in a small town near the front. While awaiting trial and lamenting their ill fortune, the two are killed during an attack on the town. It is ironic, of course, that the two soldiers die after their escape from the fighting. This irony is underscored by the memories of the younger soldier concerning his life at the front: "Short moves from damp entrenchments to dirty parapets, boring relief duty every fifteen days and a continuous, unsatisfied hunger, satiated with bread and coffee, with soup and oranges. Rumors of surrender, nocturnal desertions. . . . "[4] In short, both in "The Sergeant" and "The End of a War" Fernández Santos portrays war not as a heroic event in which the victors claim honor and fame, but as a mentally and physically destructive activity that inevitably leads to the annihilation of human existence. The characters of each story are victims of war, both in the existential sense of their frustrated desires and in the broader tragedy of their deaths.

Two other stories of *Shaved Head*, "Lejos de Madrid" [Far From Madrid] and "Mi primo Rafael" [My Cousin Rafael], are set against the backdrop of the Civil War, but are best viewed in conjunction with "Día de caza" [A Day of Hunting] and "Pecados" [Sins] as "initiation" stories. The initiation story in fiction generally centers on the experiences of young people that lead either to an important self-discovery or to the sudden acquisition of knowledge about the external world.[5] Both "Far From Madrid" and "My Cousin Rafael" portray children's initiation into the adult world through contact with the uncertainties and horrors of war. In the former story a young boy (Antonio) and his mother are vacationing near Segovia when the war breaks out and are unable to return to Madrid. The young boy's passage into adulthood results from his growing comprehension of his mother's two principal anxieties. First, since his mother evades questions concerning his father's absence, he senses that his parents would remain apart even if the war had not separated them. Second, he fears the insecurity that the war has brought to their lives and views Madrid as a refuge from the fighting. It is at the end of the story, however, when Antonio reaches the threshold of maturity. Rather than seek consolation from his mother, the roles are reversed and he offers comfort to her. Antonio cannot grasp fully his mother's despair, but in his new role as adult male he attempts to attenuate her grief.

A similar transformation from ignorance to knowledge occurs in "My Cousin Rafael," although the process transpires more abruptly and is more directly linked to the terror of war. The story again relates the evacuation of vacationers caught near the front at the beginning of the Civil War, and centers on the experiences of two young cousins, Julio and Rafael. During the course of this long narrative (fifty pages) the two boys confront a wounded soldier, are forced to seek refuge in a bomb shelter during an air raid, and stumble upon the charred body of a dead soldier. Although the boys fail to comprehend fully the implications of the fighting, the accumulation of their experiences shapes their initiation into the adult world. This process functions on two levels in the story. First of all, the two boys gain knowledge about life through their contact with the war, an idea explicitly articulated by the narrator when the family begins their evacuation and the children are treated "as if suddenly, in one night, they had become adults" (95). Beyond this, Julio must later adjust to the death of Rafael following an automobile accident. The combination of his cousin's death and the war in effect transforms Julio into an experienced adult, inured to the surrounding tragedy. Although the story presents several other complex ideas (e.g., the boredom of Julio's existence in Madrid before the war; the difficult adjustment of the families to life in Segovia), it turns upon the same underlying tragedy that shapes the meaning of "Far From Madrid": children who are suddenly confronted by an adult world that is much more complicated and painful than their own.

The other two stories that portray a sudden insight or transformation from child to adult life have no connection with the Civil War. In "A Day of Hunting" a young boy (the narrator) and his uncle go hunting in search of a chamois that is rarely spotted in the area. As the day passes we discover that the uncle had fed the boy's imagination with fantastic tales about the grandeur of the chamois, as well as with an exaggerated accounting of the events of his own life. Left alone while his uncle climbs a nearby summit, the boy sees a chamois in the distance and realizes that it is much less mysterious and majestic than his uncle's stories had led him to believe. At the same time, the boy recognizes that his uncle's tales about his life have also been exaggerated and that his happiness depends upon the propagation of lies. The process of initiation into adulthood here is the most dramatic of any of Fernández Santos's stories: the hunt (archetypal ritual of manhood) leads the narrator to maturity, but in a purely ironic fashion. Rather than from the killing of an animal, his sudden maturity stems from the realization that lying and

deceit form an important part of the adult world. He does not condemn
his uncle's actions, but simply accepts them as firmly enmeshed in the
adult way of life.

"Sins," the final initiation story of *Shaved Head*, relates the introduction of an adolescent boy to evil (as defined by the Church). As in "A Day
of Hunting," however, an ironic twist in the process shapes the youth's
view of adulthood. While taking Latin classes from an elderly priest, the
boy/narrator attends a fiesta one evening in search of diversion. The
following day the priest severely reprimands him for his sins. What was
in fact an innocent outing is completely misinterpreted by the priest,
who claims that the boy's actions represent an affront to God. As the
priest lectures him the boy focuses on the priest's bony and decrepit
hands. When the priest later dies, and the boy observes his still body,
the priest's hands again attract the boy's attention. During the following
months the narrator admits to himself that he has sinned several times in
a variety of ways, but he is haunted by the hands of the priest, which
constantly remind him of his transgressions. The sexual activity of the
narrator after the priest's death clearly initiates him into adulthood, but,
ironically, his awakening to adult sin was forged by the priest at a
moment when the boy's actions were still marked by childhood innocence.

Several other stories of *Shaved Head* revolve around child characters,
but do not center on the transformation from innocence to maturity.
"Shaved Head," for example, relates the illness of a young boy who faces
death because of an indifferent and unjust society. The thematic focus of
the story closely parallels one of the principal preoccupations of *In the
Fire*: that poverty precludes access to adequate medical care. As the
young boy's companion notes, "He is very sick. He has no money. He
can't get well because he has no money" (14). "Una fiesta" [A Fiesta] also
portrays the world of children, although in many ways (e.g., the sense of
isolation and ruin, the geographic determinism) it stands as a microcosmic rendering of the small town depicted in *The Untamed*. In the story
the men and boys of a small rural village celebrate the completion of the
harvest. The men drink and eat at the local tavern, but the boys are
excluded from the festivities even though they have worked equally as
hard as the adults. Although the boys eventually manage to steal some
wine and drink themselves into an alcoholic frenzy, the schism between
the adult and children's world is never bridged. Antonio, the oldest of
the boys, articulates the resignation and despair that characterize the
boys' view of the world: "Antonio asked himself if, as their teacher
said, there was a world in each one of those flashes of light [i.e., stars]

that shone each night, with its trees, its river and its boys working all summer long from dawn to dusk, without a single day of respite" (25–26).

The remaining stories of *Shaved Head* convey for the most part the same social/existential concerns that appear in Fernández Santos's novels of Social Realism. In "Llegar a Más" [Getting Ahead], for example, the narrative follows several years in the life of a young man who hoped to escape poverty. Through hard work he eventually achieves the status of first-class miner and earns enough money to buy a bicycle. But, as occurs with other miners in Fernández Santos's fiction (e.g., *In the Fire*, "The Story of Juana"), he is stricken by silicosis and forced to abandon his job. The writer's awareness of the plight of miners stems from an intimate familiarity with the mining areas of León and Asturias, and to his realistic portrayal of the problem he adds a powerful sense of resignation and fatalism. The title of the story reveals an ironic undercurrent, for Fernández Santos consistently suggests in his fiction that, rather than attain economic security, miners are inevitably destined to physical hardship and illness.

Two other stories that convey a fatalistic tone of resignation and despair center on the futile search for employment. In "Una vocación" [A Vocation] Fernández Santos depicts the frustrated attempts of a young announcer to secure a job at a radio station. The atmosphere of monotony and boredom that distinguishes much of Fernández Santos's early fiction forms the nucleus of the story, and clearly obstructs the youth's efforts to penetrate a stagnant system that offers few opportunities for the young. In "El doble" [The Double] the emphasis shifts to unemployment among the middle-aged, as two former bullfighters attempt to earn a living in the film industry. Both men are frustrated in their efforts, primarily because they pursue roles in fiction (i.e., they are playing bullfighters) in which they have already failed in real life. When dismissed from their jobs following an accident, they must face impending old age with scant hope of financial security or existential fulfillment.

The final story of *Shaved Head*, "Este verano" [This Summer], offers a stark portrayal of the nothingness and mental paralysis characterizing the lives of several upper-middle-class youths during summer vacation. For the most part, the youths occupy themselves with satisfying their immediate desires (primarily sexual and alcoholic). They are consumed by a vacuous and purposeless existence, yet demonstrate no keen awareness of their predicament and pursue an artificial life as if it were truly authentic. Only Pablo, after his advances are rebuffed by a young French tourist, comes to recognize the abulia that surrounds him. Although he briefly contemplates pursuing a more vital life in Madrid, Paris, or elsewhere, the reference to the cyclical pattern of time at the end of the story suggests that emptiness and boredom will continue to direct the course of his existence.

Las catedrales

Las catedrales [The Cathedrals] consists of four relatively long narratives, each prefaced by a brief descriptive fragment of an unnamed cathedral.[6] The fragment provides a short history of the particular cathedral at hand, offers a commentary on its architectural features, and describes the geographic or climatic conditions that have helped determine the nature of its existence. The impetus for structuring a collection of stories around cathedrals can be traced to Fernández Santos's work as a documentary maker. While traveling through Spain he visited nearly all of the country's important churches, and during the filming he listened to scores of stories told about the old buildings. As he related in his lecture at Salamanca: "When one makes a film documentary about a city or a monument—a cathedral, for example—it's not uncommon for a guide or an old canon, even the dean himself, to stop by with a story. . . . They relate stories, numbers, dates, sometimes legends, that pertain to the cathedral and to the people that in some way had or have a link to it. Thus, after working in several of them, I decided to collect all of those seen, heard, imagined, or lived stories in a book about cathedrals."[7]

Despite the description of a church at the beginning of each narrative, the stories of The Cathedrals cannot be categorized as religious literature. That is, they do not explore religion as an ethical, moral, or social phenomenon. In fact, religious experience scarcely figures at all in the collection, being present only to the extent that the cathedral of each story helps shape both the physical and psychological milieu. As in his two novels of this period, Fernández Santos focuses primarily on broad existential concerns and the psychological agitation that frequently accompanies the uncertain flow of memory. As noted previously, the problematic nature of time plays an important part in all of Fernández Santos's fiction, whether in the form of a stagnant and oppressive present (e.g., The Untamed and Labyrinths), or in the commingling of present and past through the free association of ideas (e.g., The Man of the Saints and The Book of Memorable Events). Hence in many respects The Cathedrals stands as a succinct compendium of the themes and techniques that shape Fernández Santos's fiction during the late 1960s and early 1970s, and anticipates his later interest in exploring Spain's distant past.

"Subida a la torre" [Climbing the Tower], the first story of the collection, revolves around a cathedral whose distinguishing characteristic is its large, single bell tower. A young woman (Inés) who grew up in the tower as daughter of the bell-ringer has returned to visit the cathedral with her husband and children after an absence of many years. As she climbs the steps of the tower, accompanied by the canon, she recalls incidents from her childhood. The first-person narration of Inés concerning the past, and the observations of a third-person narrator in the present, are interwoven throughout the story, abolishing the notion of a pure present or a pure past. This fusion of temporal planes enhances both the structural and thematic complexity of the story and demands a more active participation by the reader in order to penetrate the text. The Civil War serves as a temporal point of reference for many of Inés's memories, but the random events of her life are not evoked in chronological order. She recalls, for example, the impact of the war on her town, her brother's death during the fighting, her excursions through the cathedral with her brother, and the attempt by one of the priests to molest her on the steps of the tower. These recollections form part of her intimate consciousness and emotional experience, and their revelation as the story progresses makes her one of the most fully developed characters of Fernández Santos's short narratives.

Above all, the tower calls to mind for Inés the confinement and isolation of her youth. The tower in fact represented a prison for Inés and her family, since her father was on duty at all times, and Inés and her brother were required to return home at night before the cathedral doors were locked. It is precisely this isolation from the world that eventually leads to her marriage to Antonio. Warned by one of her friends that she will never marry if she continues to live in the church, Inés meets Antonio when he is assigned look-out duty in the tower during the war. Although few details are offered concerning their relationship, the narrative points to a sterile marriage that was spawned by convenience rather than by love and affection: "That boy has become Inés's fiancee from being [in the tower] for so long, from her washing his and his friends' clothes so much, from her warming his food and darning his socks so often. It is obvious that he became fond of her because of all that she did for him and from having her so near all day."[8]

The creation of milieu also forms an important part of the story, and is closely linked to the concept of time. While the cathedral itself stands as an imposing symbol of the continuity between past and present, the human essence that gives life and meaning to the structure has fallen victim to passing time. A mechanical carillon has eliminated the need for a bell-ringer, thus the tower no longer serves any purpose. The bell cord once used by her father hangs inert and Inés contemplates the symbolic dehumanization of her home: "The cord remains there, the same as before. Why? For what? . . . There it is. It survived everyone and nonetheless it's useless because there is no longer a bell-ringer up above and because the bells are rung from down below with an electric motor. . . . A lever is lowered, and the motor, up there, plays gloriously; another lever is touched and that motor up there, that doesn't eat, or drink, or have a wife, or Inés, or Agustinillo, becomes lifeless" (28).

This dialectic of immutability and change is also revealed in other aspects of Inés's visit to the church. The winds that once produced frightening sounds in the tower continue to haunt the building, yet no longer inspire the same fear; Inés contemplates the surrounding country-side from windows in the tower, seeing it now through mature eyes; an old owl remembered from Inés's youth still nests in the cathedral, having witnessed all of the changes that have occurred there. This blending of time periods and accumulation of memories arouses in Inés profound feelings of despair and resignation. When she and the canon reach the top of the tower, he reminds her of what he told her at the bottom: "I already told you: there's nothing left" (68). The poignant irony of the priest's statement is plainly evident, since so much of Inés's life is intimately linked to the tower. Indeed, much of her life remains there. Her visit to the cathedral thus represents a journey through time and a search for her identity, and points not to the pastness of the past, but to its infusion into the present.

The second story of The Cathedrals, "Historia del Deán" [Story of the Dean], is set in northwestern Spain in the province of Galicia. This area of the Peninsula is noted for its cold, damp weather, and within the story the backdrop of constant rain creates an atmosphere of depression and isolation. The narrative develops through the juxtaposition of two contrapuntal perspectives: that of an omniscient narrator who relates the story of the dean, and the first-person soliloquy of the dean's niece, who seeks to alleviate her despair by fantasizing about a more vital future. As occurs in "Climbing a Tower," the temporal focus of the story transcends the limits of the present, for each of the characters consciously rejects the present circumstances of his or her existence.

The elderly dean has spent most of his life studying the cathedral and its archives, and has even written articles on the building for ecclesiastical magazines. The dean's studies eventually isolate him completely from the surrounding community. He submerges himself in the past and loses touch with the present to such an extent that the present ceases to exist and to have meaning. Only the interruptions from his sister and niece, the clock on the cathedral tower, and the pocket watch on his desk remind him of temporal flow in the present. He is subsumed in the past not by the free movement of his memory, but by the conscious and deliberate probing of historical documents. When one day he loses his memory (i.e., he no longer knows where he is or what he has done), he is suddenly cut off from the past and so from meaning. Without access to history, and no longer able to escape the confines of the present, the dean's life becomes devoid of essence: "Now the night is longer because he goes to bed early . . . after a lot of walking around, a lot of observing, of meditating if life is worth living under such circumstances" (108). He dies spiritually ("It's the same as having a dead man at home, but who calls out, who asks for something now and then" [108]), and his physical death follows shortly thereafter.

The dean's niece also seeks meaning beyond the confines of the present, but does so by projecting into the future instead of probing the past. Much like Inés of "Climbing the Tower," she is a prisoner of her environment, living a lonely, oppressive existence in the small town while caring for her family. In a series of unvoiced soliloquies directed to her uncle, she reveals her frustrations and desires. She hopes to marry Joaquín, a young doctor, and move into a large house owned by her uncle in a more pleasant part of town. Like many of Fernández Santos's other characters, however, she is unable to escape the abulic circumstances that constrain her. Ultimately, therefore, she fails to realize her fantasies for the future. The brief epilogue underscores the frustrations of the niece and conveys a sense of tragic resignation. Several years after the death of her uncle, the niece and her sister pass by the house in which she once dreamed of living. The house barely remains standing, and its gardens are overgrown, untended. Clearly, like the house, the niece's fantasies have not survived the devastating effects of time.

The probing of the individual psyche and the oppressive flow of time continue to play an important role in "El largo viaje de la custodia" [The Long Journey of the Monstrance]. As in "Climbing the Tower," the evocation of the past through the free association of ideas provides insight into the principal character, helping to shape the fragmented structural design of the narrative. Related from multiple points of view, the story revolves around an unnamed fifty-five year old man charged with delivering a monstrance from his small parish church to the bishop on a nearby island. During the course of his nocturnal journey from the small island where he lives, the man recalls events from his life and reveals the abulia and resignation that define his existence. From early adolescence, when his father questioned him concerning his career goals, the protagonist felt obliged to pursue an advanced education. He abandoned his law studies after three years, however, married a girl from his small island, and took a position with the local government. His life has since progressed uneventfully, with few worries or problems. His marriage produced two sons, both of whom study at universities on the Peninsula. His job offers security, although it hardly challenges him, and he is grateful for the pattern of tranquility that life on the island provides. Yet, as he journeys to the larger island, his memories reveal a sense of incompleteness that constantly plagues him. Rather than experience a sense of failure in his life, however, the now middle-aged man feels estranged from any profound existential meaning. In his own view, his existence is best summarized via analogy with his visits to the large island: "Of all those fleeting trips [to the island] even those that he made as a man, not a friend remains. . . . Once the business of the town was taken care of, the kids examined or the monstrance delivered, no one needed him there, not even a memory, no one was going to miss him, in the same way that he didn't need the others" (161).

Time again functions as a destructive element in the story, although not through the explicit portrayal of decay and death as in "Story of the Dean." The protagonist is consistently identified as "the fifty-five year old man," an epithet which underscores the proximity of old age and the ongoing sensation of nothingness. Existential philosophy places the burden of meaning and essence squarely on the shoulders of each individual, and self-fulfillment results from the realization of what one wills to become. The fifty-five year old man of "The Long Journey of the Monstrance," however, wills nothing at all. His life thus remains stagnant, even as he is caught amid the unyielding forward flow of time.

The final story of The Cathedrals, "La ruina anticipada" [Premature Ruin], is set in contemporary Madrid against the backdrop of an unfinished cathedral. The protagonist/narrator of the story lives in the building with his family (his father is the watchman) and works as an auto mechanic in a nearby service garage. He spends each night at a local nightclub, listening to music, drinking, and attempting to meet girls. In general terms the narrator's existence reflects the life-style of many working-class Spanish youths of today, but Fernández Santos is less concerned with the narrator's social circumstances than with his existential predicament. Like the characters of *Labyrinths* or "This Summer" (of *Shaved Head*), the narrator is consumed by a pervasive tedium and abulia that divorce his existence from meaning. In contrast to the other three stories of *The Cathedrals*, in which fragmented time and memory enhance characterization and theme, "Premature Ruin" takes place entirely in the present. Nothing occurs in the story, however, that suggests a change or progression in the narrator's life. His daily routine never varies, and he remains preoccupied with the immediate gratification of his desires. The only change in his life occurs when he and his family are forced to abandon the cathedral after his sexual encounter with a young girl on the cathedral grounds. Even though he moves to another section of Madrid, however, the narrator follows the same routine as before, and the cycle of meaninglessness continues.

As in several of his other works, Fernández Santos suggests that the tragedy of the narrator's life lies not with his immediate circumstances, but with the absence of a will to act. The youth readily perceives the emptiness of his existence, and on occasion contemplates pursuing something outside the limits of his daily routine: "And beyond . . . [is] the station where trains leave for France, for the world, or wherever, for all those places where one becomes something in a short time, or at least where one tries" (193). But the lack of purpose in his life condemns him to failure, not in a social sense, but on an existential level in which being and meaning never converge. It is also in this light that the unfinished cathedral takes on significance, for the narrator's life closely mirrors the unfulfilled potential of the structure, already in ruin even before it is finished.

Paraíso encerrado

The nine short stories of *Paraíso encerrado* [Enclosed Paradise] are interwoven with an equal number of brief narrations describing Retiro Park in Madrid (i.e., the "enclosed paradise"). Each of the stories takes place at least partly within the park, and each is prefaced by a brief summary of some aspect of the park's history that relates directly to the story at hand.[9] Thus, for example, a description of the early construction of the park and the living conditions of the workers is followed by a story concerning one of the present-day employees. A brief accounting of the original gondolas for the pond leads to a story entitled "Las barcas" [The Boats]; a fragment from a seventeenth-century mandate concerning rules for the theater prefaces a narration about the comeback attempt of a middle-aged actress. Similar to the framework established in *The Cathedrals*, therefore, the descriptive fragments enhance the spatial unity of the stories and underscore the presence of the park as a powerful influence on the development of theme. As in *The Cathedrals*, the stories of *Enclosed Paradise* reveal a structural and stylistic complexity coinciding with the author's longer narrative of this period. Compared to the straightforward style of writing in his early fiction, Fernández Santos appears in these stories as a verbal voluptuary. The descriptive fragments of his narration are replete with digressions and interpolations, and his style frequently reveals a lyrical bent heretofore absent from his fiction. The commingling of past and present to form a fragmented temporal pattern also plays a crucial role in the stories. The characters explore their past both to understand the present and to seek refuge from it. Thus in some stories memory serves as a patently destructive device, while in others it evokes a time that offered happiness and hope. Throughout *Enclosed Paradise*, however, the creation of the psychological milieu is most intimately bound to Retiro Park, which serves as a spatial point of reference as well as a stimulus for the wanderings of the individual mind.

Four of the stories expose the past of individual characters as a period of deception or psychological anguish. In "Los gatos" [The Cats] the chief gardener of the Retiro seeks to escape his past by isolating himself within the protective walls of the park, spending most of his time in his small house near the animal cages, and withdrawing from social interaction with the other workers. This seclusion is irrationally motivated, of course, since it is intended to obstruct recollections of his family and the numerous political reprisals witnessed following the Civil War. The protagonist draws a parallel between the cats that inhabit his home and the obscure, but still lingering, memories. He must struggle to quell the turmoil of memory in the same way that he treats the silent cats that rest on his couch after a night of prowling: "Without stirring them up, without angering them. . . . Live as if they didn't exist."[10] The free flow of his memory, however, constantly draws the past into the present, despite his efforts to impede it. Still, the solitude of his existence offers respite from persistent anguish. In contrast to the characters of Fernández Santos's early narrative, therefore, the gardener consistently seeks to preserve his solitude, for it shelters him from the pain that he identifies with life (in time and space) beyond his immediate surroundings.

"Apartamento" [Apartment] offers a similar portrayal of destructive memories, but the principal character of the story (a middle-aged man) does not seek to annul the past. As he rests in his apartment while recovering from an illness, he contemplates the nearby park and recalls a series of incidents from his past. What he recollects, however, reveals the deception and failures that have dominated his life. Numerous sexual affairs, a ruined marriage, and lies concerning his participation in the Civil War all point to a past both destructive and painful. He is clearly aware, however, of the emptiness of his existence and his legacy of deceit. Rather than remain absorbed with the past, he demonstrates the brand of existential resignation manifested by many of Fernández Santos's characters: "The next day he would have to get up. It would be necessary to pick himself up, stand upright. He couldn't remember exactly why" (116).

In "Las circunstancias" [Circumstances] Fernández Santos links the notion of an impotent past with tedium and nothingness in the present. In a sequence of complex narrative fragments that shift between past and present, reality and fantasy, the young protagonist of the story re-creates the years of the Civil War and imagines the actions of his godfather, who evaded the fighting and suffered anguish and isolation as a result. Similar to his godfather several years before, the protagonist spends hours in the Retiro each day, hoping to escape his solitude. The random wanderings of his mind, however, subvert his intentions. Although he has barely entered adulthood, the protagonist's recollections of his past reveal an empty existence that has included drugs, unfinished studies at the university, and a love affair marked by the absence of love. This profound sense of existential failure, and the subsequent acceptance of his fate, make the protagonist of "Circumstances" a common figure among the youths of Fernández Santos's narrative. He recognizes his existence as meaningless and associates it with the similar failure of his godfather as part of an unyielding temporal flow toward nothingness: "The hours are the same, only the circumstances change. . . . My life is there. My life: waiting, smoking, humming, trembling as the useless days go by" (235–36).

"Entrevista" [Interview] is the final story in which the past appears as a destructive element. In contrast to the three stories discussed above, however, the fatalism and resignation associated with memory are mitigated by the protagonist's attempt to forge a new life to obviate the destructive power of the past. The story revolves around a middle-aged actress who is renewing her stage career after an absence of several years. As she walks through Retiro Park with the interviewer and photographer she recalls her earlier days as an actress. The interview represents a painful process of recollection for her, since it calls to mind a past defined

mainly by frustration and failure (e.g., a ruined marriage, retirement
from the stage, solitude). She resents the presence of the interviewer
both for the personal nature of his questions and for awakening memories
in her that she wishes to leave undisturbed. At the same time, however,
both the return to the stage and the interview afford her an opportunity
to foreclose upon the past and gain a new sense of commitment to the
future. Following the separation from her husband she felt "Divided,
empty, useless, alone" (143) and withdrew from the mainstream of life.
Now, however, she aims to "Start again, . . . fighting not to look back,
to keep going forward. . . . Return, make myself over within me, each
part of me, submerge inside myself each night and be reborn again the
following day" (149–50). Memory clearly plays an important role in
both the structure and theme of "Interview," but rather than preclude
the creation of a vital future, as in the previous stories, it enables the
actress to rid herself of despair and resignation. At the end of the
interview she has convinced herself of the pastness of the past, and thus
becomes "less agitated, more tranquil, softer" (150).

The fusion of past and present also forms the nucleus of three other
stories of *Enclosed Paradise*. In contrast to the narratives just discussed,
however, the past functions in these stories as a kind of paradise lost in
which memory affords refuge from the anguish and despair of the
present. In "Las bicicletas" [The Bicycles], for example, the principal
character is a middle-aged woman who visits the Retiro with her lover
Antonio. As she watches children ride their bicycles through the park
she recalls the days of her own youth and laments that her present
existence lacks the vitality of her past. As she reflects upon her past we
discover that she is unhappily married to Esteban. Although he has
provided for her financial needs, their life together is marked by routine
and boredom. She has therefore sought a lover (Antonio), but her
relationship with him has grown equally tedious. Furthermore, her
daughter (Celia) has become distant and solitary, and the two no longer
share their thoughts and emotions.

In the midst of this unhappiness the woman's recollections temporarily mitigate her despair. Above all, her youth represented a time of
undefined possibilities. Her childhood fantasies enabled her to project
herself beyond the banal realities of the moment into a virtual world
limited only by her imagination. Even her view of love was shaped by
fantasy and the reading of novels and poems. The present, in contrast,
stands devoid of possibilities and flows "without the sensation of then of
never exhausting her days, her roads, of always waiting for something

infinite, new, ineffable" (30—31). The narrative opens with the woman's entrance into the park and closes with her departure. As in several other of the stories, therefore, the Retiro provides shortlived relief from the affliction of the present. Beyond its walls, however, reality reimposes itself and the flow of time again parallels the cyclical motion of the bicycle wheels.

A second story in which a conscious longing for the past impels the character's memory is fittingly entitled "Viaje de vuelta" [Return Trip]. The narrative centers on a young man who removes himself from the collective social order and seeks refuge in the Retiro. The impetus for his withdrawal can be traced to the forced marriage of his pregnant sister, for whom he long felt an incestuous love. He spends several hours each day in the park, the location of their happy childhood escapades together. Walking by the pond and along the paths he yearns for the joy that he once felt, but which has been consumed by his sister's marriage and his own existential despair. In the present he completely rejects his sister, has abandoned his studies, and is estranged from any profound sense of meaning. Even after the marriage ends in separation he remains detached from his sister when they again walk through the park together. When viewed as part of the past, she continues to inspire his youthful fantasies. As he confronts the present, he recognizes the impossibility of regaining their childhood affection. Thus, as did the woman of "The Bicycles," the young man seeks to escape the solitude and tedium of the present by turning to the past. Eventually, however, he realizes that the past can neither be re-created nor relived.

"Los caracoles" [The Snails], the final story in which the past represents irrecoverable happiness, revolves around a broken love affair between two women. The narrative consists entirely of a monologue by the abandoned woman in which she addresses her absent lover and laments the dissolution of their love. As in several other stories of *Enclosed Paradise*, the woman evokes the past while wandering through the Retiro. The gray, rainy day, the silent cafés, and the empty chairs of the park correspond with her melancholy sentiments. In contrast to the immediate surroundings, however, the past affords the narrator temporary respite from her anguish. She recalls her frequent encounters with her lover in the park, a ski trip into the mountains, and their days together at school. In a manner that closely parallels the course of events in "Return Trip," the narrator's lover marries (primarily in order to escape poverty), but forfeits her happiness by doing so. The lives of both women are thus defined by the loss of potential fulfillment. Throughout her monologue the narrator transgresses temporal barriers out of existential necessity, and discovers that the past can be remembered, but not regained or transformed.

The remaining two stories of *Enclosed Paradise*, "El pez de nieve" [The Fish of Snow] and "Las barcas" [The Boats], deviate from the general pattern of the stories discussed above. "The Fish of Snow," the shortest narrative of the collection, parallels closely the initiation stories of *Shaved Head*. During a particularly harsh winter a young boy living in the Retiro with his family catches a tiny fish in the pond. He places the fish in a bowl and each night its bright scales illuminate the water. The young boy's imagination carries him beyond the limits of the park at night, but like the fish, which turns dull and gray in the morning, he must eventually return to the reality of his surroundings. One day in early spring the fish jumps out of the bowl, and the young boy assumes that it has returned to the pond. It is not until several years later, however, when his family is moving to a new house, that the boy discovers the decayed body of the fish stuck to the wall behind a small table: "It was no longer a fish of light, but of darkness. And the boy also had changed. . . . He was no longer a boy" (124). The young boy's initiation into adulthood has been a painful one, for he is no longer able to dream or fantasize. Indeed, his childhood imagination has been transformed into adult disillusion, and as he leaves the park for the final time he refuses to look back.

As in most of the other stories of *Enclosed Paradise*, the narrative of "The Boats" flows smoothly between past and present, but focuses less on psychological revelation than on the contrast between old and new in a constantly changing society. Two elderly workers of the Retiro, a boat caulker and a zoo keeper, sample the new plastic boats that have arrived to replace the old wooden ones. As the two men row across the pond they reminisce about the past: the Civil War, the changes in the park, their own long years of employment there. Although the story offers a somewhat simplistic dichotomy between old and new (e.g., the new plastic boats and chairs versus the wooden boats and chairs of the past; the wine at the outdoor café is "as artificial as the new boats" [202]), the essentially melancholy tone underscores the forward flow of time and the inevitability of change that will eventually displace the men from their jobs.

A orillas de una vieja dama

In contrast to Fernández Santos's previous collections of short stories, *A orillas de una vieja dama* [Within Sight of an Old Lady] is not constructed around a particular psychological or physical milieu that consolidates it into a unified whole. [11] The seven narratives that compose it vary in length from eight to eighty pages and demonstrate a diversity of style and technique that coincides with the disparate thematic focus of the stories. For example, "Pablo en el umbral" [Pablo on the Threshold] traces the early life of Picasso in Málaga, La Coruña, Madrid, and Barcelona, while "Aunque no sé tu nombre" [Although I Don't Know Your Name] and "El niño de la huelga" [The Strike Child] are set amid the upheaval and rapid transformation of contemporary Madrid. *Within Sight of an Old Lady* is less concerned with the psychological and existential problems of individuals than are *The Cathedrals* and *Enclosed Paradise*, but the fragmentation of time and free movement of memory continue to play an important part in the narrative. The stories as a group do not foreshadow a major change of direction in Fernández Santos's narrative (their very diversity precludes the establishment of a new trend), but they underscore the fundamental course of his literary development that has consistently been open to innovation and experimentation.

Despite the overall diversity of the collection, some of the stories are closely related by a common milieu or theme. "Within Sight of an Old Lady" and "Subasta" [Auction], for example, are linked by the creation of an atmosphere in which pervasive ruin and destruction in the present are contrasted with wealth and extravagance in the past. In the former story, Fernández Santos structures the narrative around the dissolution of a marriage, which in turn provokes the psychological deterioration of the scorned wife and total physical decay of her once-elegant mansion. When her husband abandons her after many years of infidelity, the woman isolates herself in the bedroom of her house. The now-idle servants recognize that they are no longer needed to maintain the household and eventually steal the furnishings and desert the woman. Left alone in the decaying house, she dies a slow death in her room.

The simplistic plot of "Within Sight of an Old Lady" belies the complexity of both the physical and psychological milieu in which it is set. Fernández Santos conveys a tragic sense of ruin and despair by forging a symbiotic relationship between the woman and the house. As the woman lies in bed, the house decays around her in the same way that her own grip on life slowly deteriorates. She hears the servants move about and detects the sound of an automobile at night, but is too far removed from the others to know that they are absconding with her possessions. Her psychological desolation fills the darkened room in which she lies, while outside the rain destroys her garden and gnaws at the crumbling statues. Driven to the edge of insanity by her insomnia, she one night leaves her bed to explore the house. Moving from room to room she realizes that the servants have abandoned her, and she returns to the confines of her bed amid vague memories of former happiness. Completely crushed by the decadence surrounding her, she finally yields to its power: "She returned to the bedroom, killed the light as if it were a bothersome or dangerous insect and, drawing the curtains, she let herself die over the period of a week; the two, woman and house, converted into a single ruin, into a single, immobile, tenacious, definitive coexistence."[12]

In "Auction" the profound sense of physical decay is less acute, but the overall milieu of ruin is intensified by the loss of fame and glory of a once-renowned actress. The woman has recently been killed in an airplane accident, and her possessions are being offered for sale at public auction. A former servant and onetime lover of the actress has returned for the sale, and as he wanders through the house he remembers the glorious past, the abrupt fall from stardom, and the gradual decline of the household, all of which are reified by the elegant furniture and personal possessions of the actress being sold to the highest bidders. No explanation is offered for the sudden reversal in the actress's fortune, although it is implied that an operation to restore her youthful appearance had much to do with it. The major focus of the story, however, lies in the disparity between the present ruin of the house and the actress's lost fame, and the way in which the servant recalls her during her days of stardom and elegant living. As in "Within Sight of an Old Lady," there is no complex portrayal of character or plot, but rather an emphasis on a ruinous ambience. The servant grows dispirited because of the decadence that surrounds him (e.g., "[the] pungent smell of dry walls, of rotten plants and furniture" [122]), but resolves at the end to remember the actress in a noble fashion: "One must know how to remember persons in the way they deserve. Even after death, one must know how to treat people like her" (123).

Two other stories are united by their focus on young adults living on the fringe of society in contemporary Madrid. In "Although I Don't Know Your Name" the first-person narration centers on a brief encounter between a young record dealer (the narrator) and a young woman who happens by his record stand at the Rastro (Madrid's large flea market). The woman has no money, has not eaten in a few days, and has clearly been taking drugs. The narrator provides her with food and offers to let her stay in his apartment. The two end up living together, but more out of convenience than emotional commitment. The woman occasionally disappears for short periods, but returns to the narrator's apartment, and the two resume their casual relationship. Eventually the narrator recognizes the need to abandon his job at the Rastro and seek more fruitful employment. Before he and the woman part, however, the woman's female lover vandalizes the narrator's apartment and destroys his recording equipment in a fit of jealous rage. As the story ends, the narrator contemplates his future while listening to a cassette recording of a song sung by the girl during their first days together.

Although the story offers no profound moral or highly developed characters, it does provide insight into the marginal existence of Spanish youths living today in Madrid. The young woman and the narrator live estranged from the mainstream of life in the capital, and their chance encounter, it is suggested, represents simply one of many experiences that will shape their lives. This same kind of estrangement in life on the fringes of society is portrayed more acutely in "The Strike Child." Also set in Madrid, the story revolves around the first-person narrator and his lover (Raquel) and their attempts to earn a living as actors. The narrator views both his profession and his own role within it with a deeply rooted cynicism and bitterness. He scorns the liberals who have organized a strike and accepts whatever work is available. By employing realistic dialogue (i.e., contemporary slang) and drawing upon his intimate knowledge of the theatrical subculture in Madrid, Fernández Santos paints a vivid picture of youthful Spanish actors searching for serious work. For the most part, however, they are forced to accept any kind of job that becomes available—in small theater cafés, in television, or the dubbing of foreign films into Spanish.

"The Strike Child" focuses primarily on the dissolution of the relationship between the narrator and Raquel. The two have been living together without any firm commitment to one another, and the narrator has no plans to make it a long-term affair. When Raquel becomes pregnant, the narrator urges her to have an abortion. She refuses, causing increased tension in their relationship. Eventually the narrator has an affair with one of Raquel's friends, while Raquel decides to pursue her future with another woman. In some ways, of course, "The Strike Child" represents an updated portrayal of the artistic crowd depicted in *Labyrinths*. The same sense of failure and tedium forms a strong undercurrent in each of the narratives, while the principal characters move through life alienated both from themselves and each other. In contrast to the artists of *Labyrinths*, however, the characters of "The Strike Child" possess a deep commitment to their art form, and the story offers less a criticism of the actors than of the circumstances that hinder their professional development. The narrator himself has fallen victim both to the seduction of the theater and to the bitter frustrations that it produces: "Sometimes you plan to leave it all, not go on tolerating it. . . . You ask yourself how you began, who persuaded you back then, and you realize that it's like getting married, you begin with illusions. . . . You're about to leave it, but where will you go? At thirty you're already old, you carry all this in your blood. . . . It must be a sickness like Jorge says. Theater ends up being just like love; the beautiful part is making it, everything before and afterward is nothing . . . " (97).

The longest story of the collection, "La sombra del caballo" [The Shadow of the Horse], also takes place in contemporary Madrid. In contrast to the other stories, however, it focuses more explicitly on the development of characters and interpersonal conflict among an upper-middle-class family. The narrative present of the story develops over a period of several months, but the past appears in fragmented form throughout and is incorporated into the present as an integral part of the characters' lives. The principal concern of "The Shadow of the Horse" lies with the relationship among a mother, her two sons (Alvaro and Pablo), and their cousin (Celia). At the beginning of the story Celia abandons her husband to take up residence in an apartment shared by the two brothers. Alvaro spends most of his time abroad, while Pablo works in Madrid for an advertising firm. As the narrative develops Pablo and Celia become lovers, but we discover through flashback sequences that it was Alvaro with whom Celia spent much of her youth and with whom she made her first sexual discoveries. Celia's affair with Pablo, therefore, results in large part from the absence of Alvaro and is impelled by her need to escape her monotonous existence. She begins to make television advertisements for Pablo's firm, but like many other Fernández Santos characters she is essentially an abulic figure, defined by her "dead eyes and dead breasts" (190). Thus, shortly after their first sexual encounter, Celia views Pablo as "already an old lover, barely accepted and already about to fade away" (179).

Although the author inserts flashbacks and employs occasional plot twists in the story, the narrative turns upon the estrangement of the characters from one another despite their physical proximity and family ties. Alvaro and Pablo remain aloof from each other due to "secret battles" (145) that are never fully explained; Pablo's mother resents him because he does not visit or call frequently; Alvaro and Celia are separated by events of their youth; Celia eventually abandons Pablo to visit a friend in California. The dissolution of the family becomes symbolically complete when their mother decides to remarry and sell the large family apartment. The living room of their home, with its old, overstuffed furniture, and the statue of a horse outside in the plaza, had always provided a feeling of stability for the family. The apartment will be transformed by the new owner, however, and only the statue outside will bear witness to the family's previous existence there. Each day the shadow of the horse follows the movement of the sun, but maintains intact the "vain memories and remote recollections" (205) of the family's past.

The two other stories of *Within Sight of an Old Lady*, "Entre nubes" [Among the Clouds] and "Pablo en el umbral" [Pablo on the Threshold], are not linked to the remainder of the collection in any technical or thematic fashion. The former is structured around a simple vignette in which a journalist and helicopter pilot fly into the mountains in search of two young climbers. The pilot is less concerned with pursuing the search than with returning to town, where he can satisfy his desire for women and wine. He agrees, however, to land near a cabin where the hikers may have sought refuge. After exploring the area, they finally find the couple inside the cabin, frozen together in an eternal embrace. A few months later, as the journalist is about to leave work, he is handed a photograph of a helicopter that has just crashed, with the pilot killed. Ironically, the reporter has only a few moments to write a brief caption for the photograph, because he is about to go out on the town. As he leaves, he recalls the pilot's appetite for sex and drinking and wonders if a woman is still waiting in a bar somewhere for the pilot to return.

"Pablo on the Threshold" consists of a pseudobiographical sketch of Pablo Picasso before his first trip to Paris in 1900. The principal outline of the story is historically accurate, and Fernández Santos offers a fictional rendering of the young painter's earliest efforts with the brush, his first public success in Barcelona, the conflict with his father over his trip to Paris, and the changing of his artistic name from Pablo Ruiz Picasso to simply Picasso. Although the story offers no new biographical data, it nonetheless provides an insightful view of Picasso's early views on art (e.g., "The great novelty of modern painting is this: any classical painter begins his painting and keeps at it, but only at the end, when he has gone over it completely, can you say that it is finished. In contrast, in a water color by Cézanne, at the first touch, the painting is there, . . . complete" [42]). The story emphasizes the importance of his stay in Horta in 1899, and the dynamic art nouveau of turn-of-the-century

Barcelona. In short, the story makes for interesting reading, and represents Fernández Santos's only experiment to date with the pseudofictional biography of a real-life figure.

Chapter Six
Conclusion

Since the early 1950s Jesús Fernández Santos has formed part of the mainstream of contemporary Spanish narrative. It would be precipitate at this time to attempt to determine Fernández Santos's ultimate niche in postwar Spanish literature, since his narrative continues to evolve and change as he matures as a writer. Certain observations can be made, however, which will elucidate the principal tenets of his fiction during the past three decades. In the first place (and perhaps most importantly), he has refused to remain stagnant in his early mode of writing—Social Realism—even though he received favorable critical attention for his role in fashioning it as an important literary movement. Rather than adhere to one particular view of the narrative process, he has followed an evolutionary path of writing impelled in part by changes in the prevailing literary environment and in part by his desire to remain faithful to his own talents and literary vision. The transformation of his narrative is characterized by the moderate assimilation of new literary modes, rather than by radical breaks with the past simply in order to imitate the experimental trends of the moment. It must be pointed out, however, that the evolution of his narrative does not imply a concurrent rejection of Social Realism, as some critics have suggested. On the contrary, several fundamental elements of his writing have remained constant (e.g., the importance of geographic determinism, a preoccupation with life in rural Spain, the powerful sense of isolation and despair) and are rooted firmly in his earliest social fiction of the 1950s.

As discussed in Chapter 1, the Neo-realist mode of writing developed as the dominant literary trend in Spain during the 1950s and early 1960s. For the most part, Fernández Santos's major narrative works of this period (*The Untamed, In the Fire, Shaved Head*) adhere to the fundamental tenets of Social Realism and focus on the outward circulation of contemporary Spanish society. Although the development of character clearly forms an integral part of his narrative, scant emphasis is placed on the psychological makeup of individuals. Instead, Fernández Santos seeks to convey the observable, "objective," aspects of society, and he does so with an elliptic style and objective narration that frequently functions as the impersonal eye of a camera. His writings focus primarily on isolated areas of rural Spain, on moribund towns and villages on the verge of dissolution. The harsh geographic and climatic conditions that consistently surround his characters in these works represent a realistic portrayal of northern Spain and contribute to the devastating sense of ruin that condemns the inhabitants to solitude and despair.

During the late 1960s and early 1970s Fernández Santos diverges from many of the literary canons associated with Social Realism. Rather than depict a collective psyche that reifies existence in rural Spain, he turns to the portrayal of individuals. Furthermore, instead of offering an objective representation of external social phenomena, he probes the existential dilemmas and psychological conflicts of his characters. Fernández Santos himself views this transformation from collective to individual characterization as a decisive moment in his development as a writer: "I believe that a qualitative change in my novels can be seen, above all beginning with *The Man of the Saints*. In my previous books, the main character was usually collective. After [*The Man of the Saints*] the characters grow more and more individualized or, to be more precise, exist in solitude, which is the only means of seeking the reason for one's own existence within oneself."[1]

Contemporary Spanish reality continues to provide the setting for Fernández Santos's fiction of this period—*The Man of the Saints*, *The Book of Memorable Events*, and the stories of *Enclosed Paradise*. Social and historical phenomena recede into the background, however, as complexity of character moves to the fore. Equally important, the uncertain flow of memory, largely absent from his earlier novels, now forms a crucial part of the narrative. Time no longer moves only forward chronologically, but rather fluctuates between past and present. Thus psychological time determines both the movement and focus of the narrative, which continually underscores the influence of the past on the present. In *The Man of the Saints*, for example, the Civil War helps shape the solitude and sense of nothingness that pervade the psyche of Antonio Salazar, even though the disaster occurred three decades before the narrative present of the novel. Likewise, the evocation of a figure from the past lays bare Margarita's psychological agitation in *The Book of Memorable Events*, while each of the stories of *Enclosed Paradise* in some fashion turns upon the commingling of past and present.

Fernández Santos's interest in extending the narrative present beyond the confines of contemporary Spain is evident to some degree in his fiction of the late 1960s and early 1970s. Present-day society still serves as the principal point of departure in these works, but often yields to moments in time that occurred decades or even a century before. In the late 1970s, however, Fernández Santos writes two novels (*The One Who Has No Name* and *Outside the Walls*) set almost entirely in the distant past. He continues to probe the psyche of individual characters in these two novels, but the milieu of medieval and baroque Spain emerges as a critical element of the narrative. From the enigmatic legend of the Dama and the mysterious life of the mountains in *The One Who Has No Name*, to the religious persecution and pseudomystical raptures of the nun in *Outside the Walls*, an ambience emerges that both complements and contrasts with the reality of current-day Spain. On the one hand, the pervasive sense of ruin and isolation of rural Spain and the despair of its inhabitants characterize life as portrayed in both the sixteenth century and the present. This is especially evident in *The One Who Has No Name*, where the narrative shuttles back and forth between postwar society and medieval times in order to reveal the cyclical pattern of life in the mountains of northern León. On the other hand, however, the historical circumstances depicted in the novels, and the manner in which the historical moment influences and molds the life of the characters, provide a sense of specificity and individuality to each of the works.

A concern for historical verisimilitude continues to influence Fernández Santos's third novel of this period, *Cabrera*. The first-person narrator of the work relates several events from the Spanish War of Independence (1808–1813) and tells of his struggle to survive amid circumstances that seem unalterably set against him. In this respect, the narrator emerges as a typical Fernández Santos character who is defeated by life itself, although the notion of raw physical survival appears with greater intensity in *Cabrera* than in any of Fernández Santos's novels to date. Less complex in its narrative structure than either *The One Who Has No Name* or *Outside the Walls*, *Cabrera* is successful in large part due to Fernández Santos's extraordinary ability to tell a good story against the backdrop of a crucial moment in Spanish history. This recurrent focusing of his narrative on the Spanish past (both in *Cabrera* and his two previous novels) leads to the creation of what Fernández Santos himself has termed a "literature of imagination." That is, he seeks to invent fictions about a distant moment in time rather than mirror and be constrained by the concrete reality of the present.

At the same time that Fernández Santos has moved consistently away from the tenets of Social Realism in terms of theme and social commitment, his manner of writing has undergone an equally dynamic evolution. The straightforward and descriptive style that marks his early fiction gradually yields to a more fluid, peripatetic mode of writing that exploits more fully the semantic and rhythmic potential of literary language. On occasion (e.g., the stories of *Enclosed Paradise*), he literally floods the page with words, achieving a stylistic complexity that contrasts sharply with his fiction of the 1950s and early 1960s. A similar transformation toward greater complexity occurs within the technical constructs of his narrative. The objective, third-person narration and the recurrent use of dialogue that characterize his early fiction do not disappear, but rather merge with first-person narration, rambling interior monologues, and fragmented temporal patterns. It must be pointed out, however, that Fernández Santos has not sought to alter his narrative style and technique in a profoundly radical way, as have many contemporary Spanish novelists and proponents of a so-called "new novel."[2] Rather than break with the past, he has constructed a new narrative atop the old, without destroying the foundations that have made his fiction consistently accessible to the reading public. As he affirmed in an interview in 1969, "I believe that the novel must be renovated, like film, painting, and music; but without losing the public, because if the public doesn't follow us, what are we going to renovate it for?"[3]

During the course of his writing career Fernández Santos has followed a pattern that coincides with many of the predominant literary fashions of his time. He has not merely imitated changing literary styles, however, but has developed a unique brand of fiction that has contributed to the growth and transformation of postwar narrative as a whole. After nearly three decades of writing novels, he has finally achieved a status that seemed elusive for so many years: he has become a well-known novelist among the general reading public, while at the same time he continues to inspire serious critical attention and scholarly analysis.

Notes and References

Chapter One

1. Although Fernández Santos asserts today that the school stifled his creative faculties and suppressed his sense of inquiry, he admits that he was forced to study and learn things there that have helped him with his writing.

2. Nearly all of the students who were able to attend the university during the early postwar years were Franco supporters and part of the newly prospering middle class. Political dissent simply was not a pressing issue for the vast majority of students.

3. Fernández Santos no longer has a copy of the play, and dismisses it as an uninteresting and immature drama. He recalls that someone from Chile asked him for a copy of it for publication in a literary magazine, but cannot remember if the play was published. I have been unable to find any reference to it in Chilean periodicals of the time.

4 After one year the magazine had twenty-seven subscribers and had sold only one hundred copies. Its demise was thus inevitable from a financial point of view.

5. Personal interview in Madrid, 26 April 1978.

6. For an overview of censorship problems in Spain during the Franco regime, and the impact of the 1966 Law of the Press, see Georgina Cisquella, José Erviti, and José Sorolla, *Diez años de represión cultural: la censura de libros durante la ley de la prensa* (Barcelona, 1977).

7. For an overview of best-selling foreign authors during this time, as well as a discussion of publishing problems faced by Spanish authors, see Fernando Alvarez Palacios, *Novela y cultura española de postguerra* (Madrid: Cuadernos Para el Diálogo, 1975).

8. Several books have been written on the evolution of the postwar novel. Among the most valuable are Gonzalo Sobejano, *Novela española de nuestro tiempo*, 2d ed. (Madrid, 1975); José Corrales Egea, *La novela española actual* (Madrid: Cuadernos Para el Diálogo, 1971); Pablo Gil Casado, *La novela social española*, 2d ed. (Barcelona, 1973); and Ramón Buckley, *Problemas formales en la novela española actual* (Barcelona: Ediciones Península, 1973).

9. Lecture delivered at the University of Salamanca, August 1971.

10. Interview, "Consulta a la novela," *Acento Cultural*, February 1959, p. 8.

11. Antonio Núñez, "Encuentro con Jesús Fernández Santos," *Insula*, nos. 275–76 (1969), p. 20.

12. *Las catedrales*, published by Seix Barral in 1970, was already in press in 1969 when Fernández Santos's dispute with the company began, and it appeared the following year. Seix Barral, however, withdrew the book from circulation shortly after it was released in response to Fernández Santos's break

with the company. The book can still be purchased today, but only on special order from the publisher. The four stories that constitute the book also appear in the author's *Cuentos completos* (Madrid, 1978).

13. Núñez, "Encuentro con Jesús Fernández Santos," p. 20.

14. Personal interview, 26 April 1978.

15. "Entrevista con Jesús Fernández Santos," *Insula*, no. 148 (1959), p. 4.

16. Lecture at the University of Salamanca, August 1971.

17. Personal interview, 26 April 1978.

Chapter Two

1. Alberto Gil Novales, review of *Los bravos*, *Insula*, no. 120 (1956), p. 6. It is important to note that *Los bravos* was a finalist in the Nadal competition in 1951, but remained unpublished until three years later.

2. Lecture delivered by Fernández Santos at the University of Salamanca, August 1971.

3. Fernández Santos has admitted on several occasions that he believes strongly in geographic determinism. He reaffirmed this belief to me in a personal interview, 26 April 1978.

4. Jesús Fernández Santos, *Los bravos* (Barcelona, 1954), p. 12. Future references to *Los bravos* are to this edition.

5. Gil Casado, *La novela social española*, pp. 244–45.

6. Sobejano, *Novela española de nuestro tiempo*, p. 325; Gregorio Martín, "Personajes en *Los bravos*: el buen samaritano," *Estudios Iberoamericanos* 2, no. 1 (1976):11–23.

7. Critics have frequently pointed to the cinematic techniques of Fernández Santos's early fiction and have concluded that his work as a film director has influenced his writing. Although cinematic techniques indeed appear in his fiction, they coincide for the most part with the general narrative trends of Social Realism as a whole and do not represent a peculiar tendency within his narrative that distinguishes it dramatically from other Social Realistic fiction of the time.

8. Jesús Fernández Santos, *En la hoguera* (Madrid, 1976), p. 129. Future references to *En la hoguera* are to this edition.

9. Sobejano, *Novela española de nuestro tiempo*, p. 329.

10. Balbino Marcos, review of *Laberintos*, *Reseña* 1 (1964):351–53.

11. J. R. Marra López, review of *Laberintos*, *Insula*, no. 214 (1964), p. 9.

12. José Battló, review of *Laberintos*, *Cuadernos Hispanoamericanos* 177 (1964):451–55.

13. Jesús Fernández Santos, *Laberintos* (Barcelona, 1964), p. 7. Future references to *Laberintos* are to this edition.

Chapter Three

1. Santiago García Díez, review of *El hombre de los santos*, *Reseña* 7 (1970): 591–93.

2. José Domingo, review of *El hombre de los santos*, *Insula*, no. 274 (1969), p. 7.

3. Carmen Martín Gaite, "Quince años después de *Los bravos*," *Estafeta Literaria*, 1 August 1969, p. 10.

4. Miguel Fernández Braso, "Jesús Fernández Santos: el novelista que vuelve a tiempo," in *De escritor a escritor* (Barcelona, 1970), p. 344.

5. Jesús Fernández Santos, *El hombre de los santos* (Barcelona, 1969), p. 84. Future references to *El hombre de los santos* are to this edition.

6. This idea closely parallels Fernández Santos's own view of life and solitude, as expressed to me in an interview in April 1978: "I believe that after a certain age one seeks out solitude. As time passes you realize, as has been said so often, that man is alone. Above all, in the crucial moments of your life you realize that *you* are alone. You have a family, friends, etc., but when the moment of truth comes, you are completely alone."

7. Domingo, review of *El hombre de los santos*, p. 7.

8. Jean-Paul Sartre, in *Existentialism from Dostoevsky to Sartre*, ed. Walter Kaufmann (New York: World Publishing Co., 1956), p. 300.

9. Jorge Rodríguez Padrón, "Jesús Fernández Santos y la novela española de hoy," *Cuadernos Hispanoamericanos* 242 (1970):437–48.

10. For a fine overview of the self-conscious novel in European and American fiction, see Robert Alter's *Partial Magic: The Novel as Self-Conscious Genre* (Berkeley: University of California Press, 1975).

11. Lecture delivered at the University of Salamanca, August 1971.

12. In his doctoral dissertation ("Jesús Fernández Santos: The Trajectory of His Fiction," University of Massachusetts, 1972), Spencer Freedman maintains that Fernández Santos focuses on the Plymouth Brethren, "an authentic Protestant community which originated in the 1820's in the British Isles" (p. 131). While the Plymouth Brethren indeed expanded their communities into Spain in the 1800s, there is no specific evidence within the novel to support Freedman's claim.

13. Lecture delivered at the University of Salamanca, August 1971.

14. Jesús Fernández Santos, *Libro de las memorias de las cosas* (Barcelona, 1971), p. 58. Future references to *Libro de las memorias de las cosas* are to this edition.

15. "Now therefore, if ye will obey my voice indeed, and keep my covenant, then ye shall be a peculiar treasure unto me above all people: for the earth is mine. And ye shall be unto me a kingdom of priests and an holy nation" (Exodus 19).

16. Fernández Santos first uses the term "literature of imagination" to describe *La que no tiene nombre* in a television interview in Madrid, 24 April 1978.

Chapter Four

1. Daniel DiNubila has shown how the ballad narrated by the servant (i.e., the ballad written by Fernández Santos) closely resembles two medieval ballads,

Romance de una fatal ocasión [Ballad of a Deadly Occasion] and *La doncella guerrera* [The Lady Warrior]. "Nothingness in the Narrative Works of Jesús Fernández Santos," Ph.D. diss., University of Pennsylvania, 1978, pp. 333—34.

2. Fernández Santos related this information to me in a personal interview, 26 April 1978.

3. Jesús Fernández Santos, *La que no tiene nombre* (Barcelona, 1977), p. 101. Future references to *La que no tiene nombre* are to this edition.

4. The verbs here are infinitives in Spanish, but not translated as such in English. Fernández Santos uses infinitives frequently in the novel to portray the tedious actions of several characters (e.g., the guerrilla, the grandson), with the same suggested meaning of static routine.

5. As reported in the Spanish daily *El País*, 8 January 1980, p. 27, *Extramuros* ranked seventh in the number of copies sold during 1979.

6. Joaquim Marco, review of *Extramuros*, *Destino*, no. 2158 (1979), p. 37.

7. María Victoria Reyzabal, review of *Extramuros*, *Reseña* 16 (1979):120—21.

8. Jesús Fernández Santos, *Extramuros* (Barcelona, 1978), p. 16. Future references to *Extramuros* are to this edition.

9. Fernández Santos seems to be aware of this problem, and thus inserts a few scenes from the trial related by an omniscient, third-person narrator.

10. This dualism between the world of the spirit and the flesh, the divine and the earthly, represents one of the most striking themes of the Spanish Baroque, and Fernández Santos captures the essence of the dilemma in the lesbian love of the two nuns.

11. See J. H. Elliott, *Imperial Spain, 1469—1716* (New York: New American Library, 1963), for a more detailed accounting of the economic and social problems of this period.

12. Ibid., p. 307.

13. For a detailed accounting of life on Cabrera during this period, see Philippe Gille, *Memoirs d'un conscrit de 1808* (Paris, 1892). For a general history of the war, see Gabriel Lovett, *Napoleon and the Birth of Modern Spain* (New York: New York University Press, 1965), 2 vols.

14. Lovett, *Napoleon*, 2:732.

15. See Gille, *Memoirs d'un conscrit de 1808*.

16. Lovett, *Napoleon*, 2:733.

17. Alexander A. Parker, *Literature and the Delinquent* (Edinburgh: Edinburgh University Press, 1967), p. 38.

18. Jesús Fernández Santos, *Cabrera* (Barcelona, 1981), p. 50. Future references to *Cabrera* are to this edition.

19. See Chapter 5 of the present study.

Chapter Five

1. See, for example, Fernández Santos's interview with Antonio Núñez, *Insula*, nos. 275—76 (1969), p. 20; his comments on Spanish television, 24

April 1978; and his discussion with me in Madrid, 26 April 1978.

2. H. E. Bates, "The Modern Short Story: Retrospect," in *Short Story Theories*, ed. Charles E. May (Athens: Ohio University Press, 1976), p. 74.

3. Ibid., p. 73.

4. Jesús Fernández Santos, *Cabeza rapada*, 2d ed. (Barcelona, 1965), p. 181. Future references to *Cabeza rapada* are to this edition.

5. Mordecai Marcus, "What Is an Initiation Story?" in May, *Short Story Theories*, pp. 189–201.

6. Antonio Iglesias Laguna has identified the cathedrals in the four stories as those in Segovia, Galicia, Santa Cruz de Tenerife, and the Almudena Cathedral in Madrid. See his review of *Las catedrales* in *Literatura de España día a día* (Madrid: Editora Nacional, 1972), pp. 377–81. It should also be noted that the fragments describing the cathedrals that preface each of the four stories have been deleted from the *Cuentos completos* edition (Madrid, 1978).

7. Jesús Fernández Santos, lecture delivered at the University of Salamanca, August 1971.

8. Jesús Fernández Santos, *Las catedrales* (Barcelona, 1970), p. 67. Future references to *Las catedrales* are to this edition.

9. The fragments that preface each story have been deleted from the *Cuentos completos* edition.

10. Jesús Fernández Santos, *Paraíso encerrado* (Barcelona, 1973), p. 62. Future references to *Paraíso encerrado* are to this edition.

11. The title of both the entire collection and the first story, *A orillas de una vieja dama* has several possible literal and connotative translations (e.g., *On the Banks {Shores} of an Old Lady*; *At the Edge of an Old Lady*, etc.). Within the context of the short story, however, the phrase is used to describe the actions and whisperings of the servants, which take place "within sight of the old lady."

12. Jesús Fernández Santos, *A orillas de una vieja dama* (Madrid, 1979), p. 21. Future references to *A orillas de una vieja dama* are to this edition.

Chapter Six

1. Josep Francesco Valls, interview with Jesús Fernández Santos, *Destino*, no. 2152 (1979), pp. 32–33.

2. There is some debate among critics concerning the existence of a "new novel" in Spain. My own view is that a new novel, with a specific theoretical foundation and set of literary canons, does not in fact exist. There can be no doubt, however, that the novel of Social Realism is no longer the dominant force in postwar fiction.

3. Miguel Fernández Braso, "Jesús Fernández Santos: el novelista que vuelve a tiempo," in *De escritor a escritor* (Barcelona: 1970), pp. 343–50.

Selected Bibliography

PRIMARY SOURCES

Los bravos. Barcelona: Ediciones Destino, 1954.
En la hoguera. Madrid: Editorial Magisterio Español, 1976; first published in 1957.
Cabeza rapada. Barcelona: Seix Barral, 2d edition, 1965; first published in 1958.
Laberintos. Barcelona: Seix Barral, 1964.
El hombre de los santos. Barcelona: Ediciones Destino, 1969.
Las catedrales. Barcelona: Seix Barral, 1970.
Libro de las memorias de las cosas. Barcelona: Ediciones Destino, 1971.
Paraíso encerrado. Barcelona: Ediciones Destino, 1973.
Europa y algo más. Barcelona: Ediciones Destino, 1977.
La que no tiene nombre. Barcelona: Ediciones Destino, 1977.
Cuentos completos. Madrid: Alianza Editorial, 1978.
Extramuros. Barcelona: Argos Vergara, 1978.
A orillas de una vieja dama. Madrid: Alianza Editorial, 1979.
Cabrera. Barcelona: Plaza & Janes, 1981.

SECONDARY SOURCES

Alborg, Juan Luis. *Hora actual de la novela española*. Madrid: Taurus Ediciones, 1968. Very positive evaluation of Fernández Santos's early fiction.
Couffon, Claude. "Recontre avec Jesús Fernández Santos." *Les Lettres Nouvelles* 6 (1958):127–32. Fernández Santos discusses his own writing and the Spanish literary environment of the 1950s.
Curutchet, Juan Carlos. *Introducción a la novela española de postguerra*. Montevideo: Editorial Alfa, 1966. Uneven study of theme and technique in *Los bravos*.
DiNubila, Daniel J. "Nothingness in the Narrative Works of Jesús Fernández Santos." Ph.D. diss., University of Pennsylvania, 1978. Valuable study of theme, style, and technique in Fernández Santos's narrative from *Los bravos* through *La que no tiene nombre*.
Domingo, José. *La novela española del siglo XX*. Vol 2. Barcelona: Editorial Labor, 1973. Brief thematic commentary on Fernández Santos's narratives through *Libro de las memorias de las cosas*.

Fernández Braso, Miguel. "Jesús Fernández Santos: El novelista que vuelve a tiempo." In *De escritor a escritor*. Barcelona: Editorial Taber, 1970. Interview with Fernández Santos and review of *El hombre de los santos*.

Freedman, Spencer G. "Jesús Fernández Santos: The Trajectory of his Fiction." Ph.D. diss., University of Massachusetts, 1972. Useful biographical overview and study of Fernández Santos's fiction through *Libro de las memorias de las cosas*.

Gaínza, Gastón. "Vivencia bélica en la narrativa de Jesús Fernández Santos." *Estudios Filológicos* 3 (1967):91−125. Very perceptive study of *Los bravos* and *En la hoguera*, but concentrates only on the tragic effects of the Civil War.

García-Viñó, Manuel. *Novela española actual.* Madrid: Ediciones Guadarrama, 1967. Provides a superficial overview of Fernández Santos's Social Realistic narrative.

Gil Casado, Pablo. *La novela social española.* 2d ed. Barcelona: Seix Barral, 1975. Useful study of the social focus of Fernández Santos's novels through *El hombre de los santos*.

Gómez de la Serna, Gaspar. "Homenaje a Jesús Fernández Santos." *Ensayos sobre literatura social.* Madrid: Ediciones Guadarrama, 1971, pp. 247−52. Brief commentary on Fernández Santos's importance as a novelist.

Martín, Gregorio C. "Personajes en *Los bravos*: El buen samaritano." *Estudios Ibero-Americanos* (Porto Alegre) 2, no. 1 (1976):11−23. Inconsistent and impressionistic study of the characters of *Los bravos*.

Nora, Eugenio G. de. *La novela española contemporánea.* Vol. 3. 2d ed. Madrid: Gredos, 1970. Brief analysis of *Los bravos* and *En la hoguera*.

Núñez, Antonio. "Encuentro con Jesús Fernández Santos." *Insula*, nos. 275−76 (1969), p. 20. Helpful interview concerning Fernández Santos's views on the novel and on writing in postwar Spain.

Rodríguez Padrón, Jorge. "Jesús Fernández Santos y la novela española hoy." *Cuadernos Hispanoamericanos* 242 (1970):437−48. Valuable review article on *El hombre de los santos*.

Schwartz, Ronald. *Spain's New Wave Novelists: 1950−1974.* Metuchen, N. J.: Scarecrow Press, 1976. Impressionistic study of theme, characters, and style of *Los bravos*.

Sobejano, Gonzalo. *Novela española de nuestro tiempo.* 2d ed. Madrid: Editorial Prensa Española, 1975. Excellent overview of Fernández Santos's narrative through *Paraíso encerrado*.

Thomas, Michael D. "Penetrando la superficie: Apuntes sobre la estructura de *Los bravos* de Jesús Fernández Santos" *Anales de la Narrativa Española Contemporánea* 5 (1980):83−90. Interesting structural analysis of *Los bravos* suggesting a thematic dialectic between hatred/vengeance and love/charity.

Tola de Habich, Fernando. Interview with Jesús Fernández Santos. In *Los españoles y el boom*. Caracas: Editorial Tiempo Nuevo, 1971, pp. 137−50.

Fernández Santos discusses his own writing and offers generally favorable comments on the contemporary Latin American novel.

Zahn, Constance Thomas. "Devitalization in Three Novels of Jesús Fernández Santos." Ph.D. diss., University of Virginia, 1976. Superficial study of social and existential factors in *En la hoguera*, *Laberintos*, and *El hombre de los santos*.

Index

Abulia, 15, 19, 22, 24, 31, 34, 37, 39, 43, 93, 103
Aldecoa, Ignacio, 3, 4
Asturias. *See* León

Bates, H.E., 94, 95
Battló, José, 31
Baum, Vicky, 5
Benavente, Jacinto, 3
Benet, Juan, 4, 69
Berlanga, Luis, 4
Buck, Pearl, 5

Castillo Puche, José Luis, 4
Cela, Camilo José, 40
Censorship, 5
Collective Protagonist, 12, 14, 22, 32, 92
Critics' Prize, 40
Cruz, San Juan de la, 78

Delibes, Miguel, 40
Domingo, José, 40, 43
Dos Passos, John, 3

Existentialism, 15, 23, 26–28, 36–37, 38, 40–64, 65, 81, 87, 88, 89, 99, 104, 105, 107, 110, 114, 118

Faulkner, William, 3
Fernández Santos, Jesús: and Spanish Civil War, 1–3, 6; and film, 4, 8–9, 53–54, 100, 122n7; and literary ambience of postwar, 6–8; and literary formation, 3–4

WORKS: NOVELS
Book of Memorable Events, The (Libro de las memorias de las cosas), 9, 53–64, 65, 70, 75, 81, 88, 94, 100, 118
Cabrera, 64, 85–93, 119
In the Fire (En la hoguera), 6, 22–31, 32, 38, 39, 40, 42, 50, 69, 70, 81, 88, 95, 98, 99, 117
Labyrinths (Laberintos), 8, 31–39, 40, 46, 100, 105, 113
Man of the Saints, The (El hombre de los santos), 7, 9, 40–53, 62, 63, 64, 65, 75, 84, 88, 94, 100, 118
One Who Has No Name, The (La que no tiene nombre), 9, 64, 65–75, 76, 81, 85, 92, 94, 119
Outside the Walls (Extramuros), 64, 75–85, 93, 94, 119
Untamed, The (Los bravos), 5, 6, 9, 11–22, 23, 31, 32, 38, 39, 40, 41, 42, 50, 62, 63, 65, 69, 74, 81, 95, 98, 100, 117

WORKS: PLAYS
While the Rain Falls (Mientras cae la lluvia), 3

WORKS: SHORT STORIES
"Although I Don't Know Your Name" ("Aunque no sé tu nombre"), 111, 112–13
"Among the Clouds" ("Entre nubes"), 115
"Apartment" ("Apartamento"), 106–107
"Auction" ("Subasta"), 111, 112
"Bicycles, The" ("Las bicicletas"), 108–109
"Boats, The" ("Las barcas"), 105, 110

Cathedrals, The (*Las catedrales*), 9, 64, 94, 100–105, 107, 111
"Cats, The" ("Los gatos"), 106
"Circumstances" ("Las circunstancias"), 107
"Climbing the Tower" ("Subida a la torre"), 101–102, 103
"Day of Hunting, A" ("Día de caza"), 96, 97, 98
"Double, The" ("El doble"), 99
Enclosed Paradise (*Paraíso encerrado*), 64, 94, 105–10, 111, 118, 120
"End of a War, The" ("El final de una guerra"), 95, 96
"Far From Madrid" ("Lejos de Madrid"), 96, 97
"Fiesta, A" ("Una fiesta"), 98
"Fish of Snow, The" ("El pez de nieve"), 110
"Getting Ahead" ("Llegar a más"), 99
"Interview" ("Entrevista"), 107–108
"Long Journey of the Monstrance, The" ("El largo viaje de la custodia"), 103–104
"My Cousin Rafael" ("Mi primo Rafael"), 96, 97
"Pablo on the Threshold" ("Pablo en el umbral"), 111, 115–16
"Premature Ruin" ("La ruina anticipada"), 104–105
"Return Trip" ("Viaje de vuelta"), 109
"Sergeant, The" ("El sargento"), 95, 96
"Shadow of the Horse, The" ("La sombra del caballo"), 114–15
Shaved Head (*Cabeza rapada*), 8, 94, 95–100, 110, 117
"Shaved Head" ("Cabeza rapada"), 98
"Sins" ("Pecados"), 96, 98

"Snails, The" ("Los caracoles"), 109–10
"Story of the Dean" ("Historia del Deán"), 102–103, 104
"Strike Child, The" ("El niño de la huelga"), 111, 113–14
"This Summer" ("Este verano"), 99, 100, 105
"Vocation, A" ("Una vocación"), 99
Within Sight of an Old Lady (*A orillas de una vieja dama*), 64, 94, 110–16
"Within Sight of an Old Lady" ("A orillas de una vieja dama"), 111–12

Fictional history. *See* Literature of imagination
Fraile, Medardo, 3, 4
Franco, Francisco, 1, 66, 69

García Díez, Santiago, 40
García Lorca, Federico, 3
Geographical Determinism, 10, 12, 13, 16, 24, 32, 41, 42, 65, 69–70, 81, 82, 84
Gil Casado, Pablo, 19
Gil Novales, Alberto, 11
Goldoni, Carlo, 3

Hemingway, Ernest, 3

Initiation Story, 88, 96, 97, 98, 110
Intrigue, 12, 21, 22, 29, 63, 74

Latin American Novel, 7
Law of the Press. *See* Censorship
León, 1, 9, 10, 11, 22, 65, 66, 67
Literature of imagination, 64, 65–93, 119

Marco, Joaquim, 75

Marcos, Balbino, 31
Marra López, J.R., 31
Martín, Gregorio, 19
Martín Gaite, Carmen, 4, 40
Memory. *See* Time

Nadal Prize, 5, 53
Neo-realism. *See* Social realism

Paso, Alfonso, 3

Revista Española, 4, 5
Roberts, Cecil, 5
Rodríguez Moñino, Antonio, 4, 5
Rodríguez Padrón, Jorge, 50
Rulfo, Juan, 69

Sánchez Ferlosio, Rafael, 3, 4
Sartre, Jean-Paul, 45
Sastre, Alfonso, 3, 4
Saura, Carlos, 4
Sobejano, Gonzalo, 19, 25
Social Criticism, 29−30, 82−84, 98, 99

Social Realism, 6, 11−39, 40, 50, 51, 53, 62, 64, 65, 94, 117
Spanish Civil War, 1−3, 6, 13, 22, 33, 41, 43, 44, 45, 46−47, 55, 61, 66, 73, 95, 96, 101, 106, 107, 118
Steinbeck, John, 3
Strindberg, August, 3

Teresa de Jesús, Santa, 78
Time, 13, 14, 15, 31, 36, 44−47, 70−72, 77, 78, 101, 102, 103, 104, 106, 107, 108, 109, 110, 118, 119

Vargas Llosa, Mario, 40

Williams, Tennessee, 3
Wasserman, Jacob, 15, 17

Zweig, Stefan, 5